BESSIE HEAD, one of Af[...]born in South Africa [...]between a black man and a [...]one, and she drew heavily upon her own personal experiences for her novels. She was sent to a foster family until she was 13, and then a mission school before training as a teacher. After a few years teaching she left to work as a journalist for *Golden City Post*, a DRUM publication but an unsuccessful marriage and her involvement in the trial of a friend lead her to apply for another teaching post, in Botswana, where she took up permanent exile. She remained there, with the precarious status of 'refugee', for 15 years before she gained citizenship in 1979, and it was in Botswana that Bessie Head died tragically early, aged 49, in 1986.

Botswana is the backdrop for all three of her outstanding novels. *When Rain Clouds Gather*, her first novel, based on her time as a refugee living at the Bamangwato Development Farm, was published in 1969. This was followed by *Maru* (1971) and her intense and powerful, autobiographical work *A Question of Power* (1973). Her short stories appeared as *The Collector of Treasures* in 1977, and in 1981, *Serowe: Village of the Rain Wind* was published, a skilful and original historical portrait of 100 years of the Botswanan community, reconstructed through the words of different members of the village and *A Bewitched Crossroad*, appeared in 1984. *A Woman Alone* (1990), a collection of Bessie Head's autobiographical writings, and *Tales of Tenderness and Power* (1990), a moving selection of famous and previously unpublished works, have been published posthumously. All her works (except for *A Bewitched Crossroad*), are available in the Heinemann African Writers Series.

CRAIG MACKENZIE completed an MA on the life and work of Bessie Head in 1985. Since 1987 he has worked as a researcher at the National English Literary Museum in Grahamstown, South Africa. His publications include the monograph *Bessie Head: An Introduction*, critical articles on Bessie Head, as well as more general articles on the South African short story.

BESSIE HEAD

A WOMAN ALONE

Autobiographical writings

Selected and edited by Craig MacKenzie

HEINEMANN

Heinemann Educational Publishers
Halley Court, Jordan Hill, Oxford OX2 8EJ
a division of Reed Educational & Professional Publishing Ltd

Heinemann: A Division of Reed Publishing (USA) Inc.
361 Hanover Street, Portsmouth, NH 03801-3912, USA

Heinemann Educational Books (Nigeria) Ltd
PMB 5205, Ibadan
Heinemann Educational Boleswa
PO Box 10103, Village Post Office, Gaborone, Botswana

MELBOURNE   AUCKLAND
FLORENCE   PRAGUE   MADRID   ATHENS
SINGAPORE   TOKYO   SAO PAULO
CHICAGO   PORTSMOUTH (NH)   MEXICO
IBADAN   GABORONE   JOHANNESBURG
KAMPALA   NAIROBI

British Library Cataloguing in Publication Data

Head, Bessie
A woman alone
I. Title   II. Series
823 [F]

ISBN 0-435-90578-3

Series Editors:
Chinua Achebe 1962-1990
Adewale Maja-Pearce 1990-94

Series Consultant: Abdulrazak Gurnah 1994

Photoset by Wilmaset, Birkenhead, Wirral
Printed and bound in Great Britain by
Cox & Wyman Ltd, Reading, Berkshire

97   98   99   10   9   8   7   6   5

CONTENTS

For my wife Susan
and with thanks to
Stephen Gray

INTRODUCTION

The task of mapping the life of an author, however prosaic that life may be, is something most literary biographers approach with a great deal of caution. This is the case even if the intention is to vilify the author concerned, for the most vapid life story must nevertheless hold within itself countless imponderables – a myriad dark, inchoate childhood experiences that fashion the adult personality.

The life of Bessie Head was anything but prosaic, and it certainly had its share of imponderables. Her origins, to begin with, are ambiguous at best. Her early life is a blur of pain and uncertainty. Little is known about her marriage and the reasons for its breakdown. In fact it is only with her arrival in the literary world in the seventies and the relative stability this created that her life begins to take on familiar contours. Even then, most of the details have their source in the author herself, and independent corroboration of basic facts is hard to come by. She proved to be an unreliable witness to her own life, often contradicting herself in interviews, and the chief source of biographical data – her first three novels – present her life filtered through her rich but necessarily inventive literary imagination.

Whatever the uncertainties, the task of mapping the life of an author like Bessie Head undoubtedly becomes an investigation into the enigma of human prejudice. For in the process of unravelling the strands of her anguished life story one encounters instances of immense suffering and privation, crippling alienation, and perhaps most of all, personal confusion. It is this personal confusion (no doubt wrought by the bureaucratic callousness of a regime that legislates against people of colour) that is at the centre of Bessie Head's troubled life.

It is not my task, however, to offer a definitive version of the life of this remarkable woman. That would clearly pre-empt what is to follow. The intention behind this book is to allow the author the opportunity to tell the story of her own life, and to offer the reader a collection of illuminating although sometimes contradictory writings that span the entire productive period of her life. Of course, there has been a certain amount of editorial intervention, and it is therefore perhaps necessary to sketch a brief map of her life in order to explain the rationale behind the arrangement of the writings that make up this collection.

The pieces are arranged roughly chronologically – from 1962 to 1985 (the years during which they were written) – and are divided into three periods, each of which is introduced by an autobiographical passage in which the author sets the scene to the period which follows. The idea is that these introductory passages provide a narrative thread which links the three major periods of her life: her early life in South Africa (1937–1964), her period of exile in Botswana (1964–1979) and, finally, her life as a Botswanan citizen (1979–1986). While it must be acknowledged that other groupings could be argued for (for example, on the basis of the trends in her writing: (i) early journalism, (ii) introspective novel-writing and (iii) socially oriented stories, interviews and histories) there is substantial biographical backing for the divisions in the present collection.

Indeed, the focus is not principally on the writer Bessie Head's *oeuvre* but on the life of a South African-born woman who happened to become an internationally recognised author. The writings that make up this collection, in other words, are intended as a 'piece-meal' portrait of this life, a mosaic of sketches, essays and personal notes – making the present work primarily a biographical (as opposed to critical) study.

As a South African-born 'Coloured', Bessie Head was subjected to all the brutalities meted out to those citizens not born white, and she, as a 'first generation' child of bi-racial origin, bore the full brunt of South Africa's discriminatory legislation. Her place of birth, foster childhood, adolescence as an orphan, her failed marriage and experiences as a 'non-white' in the various ghettos around the cities of South Africa form the background to the first phase into which this volume is divided.

A clear break comes with her departure for Botswana on an exit permit. South Africa becomes something of the past, a nightmare-world she is eager to forget. In her autobiographical third novel, *A Question of Power* (Heinemann, 1974), which is pivotal to any examination of her life and work, she describes her feelings about South Africa in this way:

> She hated the country. In spite of her inability to like or to understand political ideologies, she had also lived the back-breaking life of all black people in South Africa. It was like living with permanent nervous tension, because you did not know why white people there had to go out of their way to hate you or loathe you. They were just born that way, hating people, and a black man or woman was just born to be hated. There wasn't any kind of social evolution beyond that, there wasn't any lift to the heart, just this vehement vicious struggle between two sets of people with different looks . . . (p.19)

Botswana became a new beginning, although as a refugee from South Africa she was not officially made welcome. And, indeed, her troubles did not end with her arrival in Botswana. Around 1969 she suffered a lengthy and debilitating nervous breakdown. This may have been congenitally induced. Her mother appears to have suffered from a progressive psychosis, and Bessie was throughout her life acutely conscious of the fragility of her mental balance. *A Question of Power* describes in graphic and disturbing detail the harrowing process of her mental breakdown. At one point in the novel (and in her life) she accuses Sir Seretse Khama of ritual cannabilism and incest and posts these accusations outside the post office in Serowe. This marked the real onset of madness and she was taken into psychiatric custody. Her breakdown appears to have occurred in the form of sporadic attacks which were spread over a period of two years. When she emerged, however, it was with a reconstituted sense of self, a new resolve and a firmer grip on the world. This is how *A Question of Power* ends:

She had fallen from the very beginning into the warm embrace of the brotherhood of man, because when a people wanted everyone to be ordinary it was just another way of saying man loved man. As she fell asleep, she placed one soft hand over her land. It was a gesture of belonging. (p.206)

The third phase into which I have divided her life (1979 – 1986) was heralded by her securement of Botswanan citizenship. In 1977 she had applied for citizenship and was turned down. A new sense of alienation began to develop within her, and in an interview with Jean Marquard in the same year, she said bitterly,

I have liked Botswana very much although I have got nothing out of loving a country that didn't want me.[1]

In 1979, however, she was granted Botswanan citizenship, and was able to travel to Germany for the Africa Festival on a Botswanan passport. She had never re-applied for citizenship, and could only put the government's change of heart down to her international success as a writer, and as a *Botswanan* writer, moreover. In 1982 she was invited to Gaborone to give a special lecture and to participate in a book-signing at an official exhibition on 'Writers of Botswana'.

Clearly, this last phase of her life was important. From her new vantage point as recipient of local and international accolades she could now look back and put her life into a meaningful perspective. The publication of her eulogistic social history *Serowe: Village of the Rain Wind* in 1981 and her 'major obsession, the Khama novel'[2] *A Bewitched Crossroad* in 1984 (research for both of which had begun in the early seventies), was the culmination of a long, hard battle for acceptance. Her death in 1986 was premature, a foreshortening of what could otherwise have been a long and rewarding relationship as a citizen with her adoptive country Botswana. With what might have been extraordinary prescience, she said of her last novel:

I am trying to gather several threads together to create a feeling of continuity in my work . . . to finally record some of the kind of welding I felt on coming to a country like Botswana. It was like

xii

finding roots and these roots really go back, for me, to the old tribal way of life and its slow courtesies . . . So this final work I am on will have the effect of rounding off my Southern African experience. I think I will then let it fall asleep in my mind.[3]

The generic classification of the pieces in this volume poses a challenge to the literary critic. They span a number of overlapping genres: letters, journalism, autobiography, fictional sketches, essays, forewords, explanatory notes on novels. Were one to assume these generic markers to denote discrete and insular categories, it would appear possible to label the pieces in the present volume accordingly. At the end of this exercise, however, one would be left with a number of alarming and messy anomalies: how could 'Snowball: a story' be classified a fictional sketch when three quarters of the piece is devoted to the author's reflections on her day-to-day life in District Six? And why does the piece 'An African Story' (so misleadingly titled) fall into neither of the categories 'fictional sketches' or 'journalism', or even wholly into 'autobiography' for that matter? Its title promises fictional narrative, and indeed it begins like a story, but then quickly becomes autobiographical, even anecdotal, and ends with a philosophical reflection on the future of South Africa. And this indeterminacy characterises almost every piece included in the present volume.

The truth is that the majority of the pieces assembled here defy classification. At their two extremes they represent autobiography and (very nearly) pure fiction. Most of them are however strung somewhere between these two extremes, and each (with a few exceptions) represents an amalgam of self-reflection, semi-fictional narrative, journalistic reportage and cultural comment. The significance of each piece (and the justification for its inclusion in the present volume) is that it reveals something about the extraordinary life of the author Bessie Head.

It would perhaps be useful to include at this point a brief background to the pieces collected together in this volume. This involves, to some degree, a discussion of the entire body of Bessie

Head's published writing, of which the present collection represents only a small part. ᶜᵒ ᵗʰᵉ ˢˢ ā²

Her contribution to the seminal periodical *The New African* is important because it is an early example of what was to become a constant feature of her unusual life: her similarity with, but also divergence from other writers of her generation. Like Maimane, Matshikiza, Themba, Nkosi and Mphahlele, who also contributed articles and stories to *The New African*, she was a writer of the sixties: educated, articulate, and well read. Yet while all of them are stylistically categorised as part of the 'Drum School', her writing was even then significantly different both in style and substance. Where the *Drum* writers are noted for their racy, worldly-wise, often sensationalist journalistic style, accompanied (certainly in their articles for *The New African*) by an overtly political content, Head from the very start adopted a personal, 'apolitical' approach. She was on the periphery of the *Drum* world, and in fact, before coming down to Cape Town in 1960, wrote for a newspaper called *Golden City Post* (later simply *Post*), which was a DRUM publication and not a part of *Drum* magazine itself. Nevertheless, like her *Drum* contemporaries, she considers her later writing to have been influenced by her association with that milieu: cutural surroundings

> With journalistic demands you produce short stories every day under tremendous pressure with a deadline for the newspaper. I feel that that background of journalism benefitted me later for my particular kind of style. I am not loose and baggy. I'm very concise and taut, and I intend saying as much as possible in the most economical way.[4]

Her very first piece for *The New African* was, uncharacteristically, a poem. It has an angry, almost aggressive tone, and is clearly an expression of extreme frustration. It begins in the following way:

> I am Black.
> Okay?
> Hot sun and the geographical set-up

Made me Black;
And through my skin
A lot of things happen to me
THAT I DON'T LIKE.
And I wake each morning
Red murder in my eyes
'Cause some crook's robbed me again,
Taken what little I had right out of my hands
With the whole world standing by
And doing nothing . . .
Okay?[5]

The poem is not included in this collection because of its disparity
with the other pieces in terms of literary quality as well as generic
category, but it does show a young writer grappling with a tangle
of words and emotions for which she has no coherent means of
expression. In her next piece for *The New African*, 'Let me tell a
story now . . .' (reproduced in this collection), she acknowledges
this inarticulateness:

When I think of writing any single thing I panic and go dead
inside.

Significantly she adds:

Perhaps it's because I have my ear too keenly attuned to the
political lumberjacks who are busy making capital on human
lives.

Twelve years later, in 'Some notes on novel writing', she was to
remark:

The environment [South Africa] completely defeated me, as a
writer.

It is this early suspicion of politics and politicians (confirmed in
this last remark) that marks her writing off from that of her
contemporaries. From the start she set herself on a path that was
uniquely her own. The angry tone of her first published piece of
writing was atypical: all of the writing that followed is character-

ised by its moral depth, sensitivity and understanding. In fact, her whole philosophy is summed up in these words (from 'Some notes on novel writing'):

> the immense suffering black people experience in South Africa . . . created in me a reverence for ordinary people.

Other contributors to *The New African* included James Matthews and Richard Rive, both of whose writing is generally considered part of the cultural milieu of Cape Town's District Six. And while it was here that Bessie lived during the time that she contributed her first six pieces for *The New African*, it is incorrect to consider her writing, either at that time or later, a part of that milieu. She did not speak Afrikaans, the language of the 'Cape Coloured', and only lived in District Six for about three and a half years while in her twenties. Its distinctive ambience was not therefore a formative influence on her later writing – although it undoubtedly played a role in fashioning her 'reverence for ordinary people'.

Perhaps the most significant aspect of her early writing for *The New African* was that it made her politically suspect in the eyes of the authorities. One need only note the fate of her fellow contributors to divine the official view of the *The New African*: Todd Matshikiza died in exile after being banned under the Suppression of Communism Act; Ezekiel Mphahlele went into exile for twenty years; Arthur Maimane is still in exile in London; Dennis Brutus is still in exile in America after being jailed on Robben Island; Bloke Modisane died recently in exile after being banned under the Communism Act. Can Themba, Jonty Driver, Lewis Nkosi, Breyten Breytenbach – the list is endless. Of course it was not solely due to the fact that they wrote for *The New African* that these writers were persecuted in this way, but their common fate does say something about the political orientation of the magazine and its reception by the authorities. When Bessie applied for a passport to travel to Botswana she was refused, and attributes this (at least in part) to her writing for *The New African*.

Like many of her 1960s contemporaries it was due to these sorts of social and political pressures that she left South Africa in March *cảnh thành?*

1964 for exile in Botswana. And yet, unlike them, she took root in her new environment, and made it her own:

> The least I can ever say for myself is that I forcefully created for myself, under extremely hostile conditions, my ideal life. I took an obscure and almost unknown village in the Southern African bush and made it my own hallowed ground. (Preface to 'Witchcraft'.)

Very soon after arriving in Botswana her first tribute to her adopted village appeared: 'For Serowe: a village in Africa' (October 1965). This set the tone for many of the pieces that followed. The sense of Botswana's almost uninterrupted African history had an immediate and profound influence on her, a victim of almost total deracination in the land of her birth.

However, an urgent tone had already entered her writing with the publication of 'The green tree' in October 1964[6], and this strain surfaced insistently among the more composed pieces until *A Question of Power* appeared in 1973. The publication of this cathartic, autobiographical novel signalled a major shift in her orientation. She goes on from this point to explore the lives of her fellow Serowan villagers in a collection of stories, *The Collector of Treasures* (1977), a social history, *Serowe: Village of the Rain Wind* (1981), and an historical novel, *A Bewitched Crossroad* (1984).

◇

bất đắc, việt

With rising literacy in Botswana the impact of the written text is increasingly going to be felt and, clearly, Bessie Head's importance as a writer of Botswana will grow. I understand that, following her death in 1986, the Botswanan authorities are constructing a building in Serowe to house and exhibit the Bessie Head papers. Something else of interest is that foreign volunteer workers are given her first novel, *When Rain Clouds Gather*, which deals fairly extensively with agriculture in Botswana, to orient themselves to their new environment. Finally, prior to travelling up to Serowe to visit Bessie in early 1985 I was gratified to discover a bookshop in Gaborone in which three bookcases were entirely *no bat, xvatchy*

devoted to multiple copies of her works. Her prominence as a local writer was proudly displayed in this way.

All this indicates that the importance and influence of Bessie Head as a Botswanan author is going to be felt, not only abroad, where her work has for a long time had an enthusiastic audience, but also back here in Southern Africa generally, and of course, in Serowe particularly. *add*

The memory that remains with me from that visit in 1985, however, is of a small, vital woman with a crippling legacy of loneliness and rejection, eking out an existence in a quiet corner of Africa. She had lived a good deal of her childhood and early adulthood in the cities of South Africa; she was an author whose works have been translated into several European languages, who *called* has been hailed the finest woman novelist in Africa, who has been offered citizenship of Norway and numerous trips abroad, all expenses paid. And here she was, a woman alone with her son, living in a two-roomed dwelling without the convenience of electricity or plumbing.

In a perceptive article on the author for *Africa Now*, Lorna de Smidt writes:

> Bessie Head has already given her thanks to Serowe in the tender and vivid biographical account of its people and their history . . . maybe some day, someone will in turn attempt a biography of this remarkable woman.[7]

This volume is intended as a first step towards the publication of that biography.

Craig MacKenzie
Grahamstown 1989

1 **Marquard, Jean.** 'Bessie Head: exile and community in Southern Africa.' *London Magazine* 18.3&4 (1978/79): 51–52.
2 **Head, Bessie.** 'A bewitched crossroad.' *The Bloody Horse* No.3 (Jan./Feb. 1981): 5.
3 **Beard, Linda Susan.** 'Bessie Head, Cape Gooseberry and the question of power.' *ALA Bulletin* 12.2(1986): 41.

4 **See MacKenzie, Craig and Cherry Clayton, eds.** *Between the Lines:
Interviews with Bessie Head, Sheila Roberts, Ellen Kuzwayo, Miriam Tlali.*
Grahamstown: National English Literary Museum, 1989: 8.

5 **Head, Bessie.** 'Things I don't like'. *The New African* 1.7(1962): 10.

6 **Head, Bessie.** 'The green tree'. *Transition* 16.4(1964): 33. This
fictional piece is not reproduced in this collection.

7 **De Smidt, Lorna.** 'Where rain is paramount.' *Africa Now* Vol.7
(Oct.1981): 102.

NOTE ON THE TEXT

The autobiographical preface to the story 'Witchcraft' (which first
appeared in *Ms.* magazine) and the *Drum* piece 'Notes from a quiet
backwater' have each been divided into two parts in order to enhance
the narrative structure of this collection. Nothing was omitted from
either of these pieces.

In 'An unspeakable crime' and 'A gentle people' references which
were made to an individual's name have been dropped.

In 'Letter to *Transition*' and 'A note on *Rain Clouds*' references which
were made to extraneous material of no interest in the present context
have been omitted.

All of the remaining pieces are reproduced unchanged except for
minor typographical errors.

I was born on the sixth of July, 1937, in the Pietermaritzburg Mental Hospital, in South Africa. The reason for my peculiar birthplace was that my mother was white, and she had acquired me from a black man. She was judged insane, and committed to the mental hospital while pregnant. Her name was Bessie Emery and I consider it the only honour South African officials ever did me – naming me after this unknown, lovely, and unpredictable woman.

from **Preface to 'Witchcraft' 1975**

1

Beginnings:

South Africa
1937–1964

Notes from a quiet backwater I

There must be many people like me in South Africa whose birth or beginnings are filled with calamity and disaster, the sort of person who is the skeleton in the cupboard or the dark and fearful secret swept under the carpet.

The circumstances of my birth seemed to make it necessary to obliterate all traces of a family history.

I have not a single known relative on earth, no long and ancient family tree to refer to, no links with heredity or a sense of having inherited a temperament, a certain emotional instability or the shape of a fingernail from a grandmother or great-grandmother.

I have always been just me, with no frame of reference to anything beyond myself.

I was born on July 6, 1937, in the Pietermaritzburg mental hospital. The reason for my peculiar birthplace was that my mother was white and my father black.

No details were ever available about my father beyond the fact that he worked in the family stables and took care of their racehorses.

A great deal became known to me about my mother when I was thirteen.

At birth I had been handed to a Coloured foster mother to whom I became deeply attached and accepted as my mother. She was paid a pittance of three pounds a month to care for me.

There was sly, secret supervision of my life, which was unknown to me. Each month a social worker turned up with a notebook to jot down notes and records of my day-to-day existence.

When I was thirteen the foster mother fell into a state of abject poverty and a decision was made to transfer me to a mission orphanage in Durban.

Problems arose when the school holidays came round.

I was called to the office of the principal, a British missionary, who announced curtly: 'You are not going back to that woman. She is not your mother.'

A teacher found me lying prostrate and at the point of collapse

3

under a bush in the school garden. On asking what was the matter, I told her I was about to die as no one would let me go home to my mother.

Thereupon the principal bundled me into her car and for some strange reason raced straight to the Durban Magistrate's Court where a magistrate read something out to me in a quick gabble that I did not hear or understand.

But he looked at me accusingly as though I were some criminal and said, hostilely: 'Your mother was a white woman, do you hear?'

On arriving back at the mission, the missionary opened a large file and looked at me with a wild horror and said:

'Your mother was insane. If you're not careful you'll get insane just like your mother. Your mother was a white woman. They had to lock her up as she was having a child by the stable boy who was a native.'

The lady seemed completely unaware of the appalling cruelty of her words. But for years and years after that I harboured a terrible and blind hatred for missionaries and the Christianity which they represented, and once I left the mission I never set foot in a Christian church again.

But it was also the lady's delight whenever she had a problem with me to open that file and read out bits of it. So I gained a hazy impression of my beginnings, of a pathetic letter written by my mother in the mental hospital, stipulating that above all things, it was her earnest desire that I receive an education and that some of her money should be set aside for my education, of a period of emotional instability and depression in her life that had led her to inflict a terrible disaster on herself.

She had been married and when the marriage fell through she returned to the family home.

In a sudden and quite unpredictable way she decided to seek some love and warmth from a black man. But the family belonged to the top racehorse owning strata of South African society.

The family home was Johannesburg and it was necessary for them to hide their skeleton in the cupboard far away from home.

4

She never came out of the mental hospital in Pietermaritzburg and died there in 1943.

In contrast to all this I fear any biographer would be bored to tears by my own life story. There are truly no skeletons in my cupboard or dark secrets swept under the carpet; no real sensation or scandal has ever touched my life and I look back on myself as a personality, plain and ordinary, without any glamour or mystery.

1982

Let me tell a story now . . .

◆

I don't know why this is so but the first thing a person you've just been introduced to will ask you is: 'What work do you do?' I don't mean that he or she will ask it bluntly, just like that. They will hedge around a bit but eventually they will get down to the point and drag it out of you. As I say, I don't know why you dare to ask such a personal question but the reason that I do is because each person that I meet is a complete mystery to me. I have to find a quick and superficial way of piecing him together so that I know where I stand. I mean, I don't like to behave like a fool and some people instantly give you the feeling that you are behaving like a fool. I'm specifically referring to a hard case lawyer I once knew. I struggled quite unsuccessfully to explain a delicate matter to him that needed just a bit of understanding and humane feeling and couldn't understand why he kept pulling me to shreds. Only later I learnt that the man's mind worked this way: 'Let's consider it on a judicial basis.' The poor man had completely identified himself with his work. He was all one-sided. A very dangerous type that because they can bust your ego to bits and you won't know what's happening to you, especially if your enemies are around and watching the terrific beating you are taking from one who knows all the answers.

In a broad sense then I would say a person's character type makes him gravitate to a certain type of work. The fussy-fussy,

5

jumpy sort of woman becomes a typist where she can mess around all day minding other people's businesses. The rather heartless, dominating you-actually-deserve-all-you-get type becomes a social worker. The tough guy with sadistic tendencies becomes a jail warder or a policeman. The dull, drab and toiling type a waitress, shop-girl or nurse. And so on.

I'm sorry but it has taken me quite a long time to get down to what I actually wanted to say. When anyone asked me this question, namely: 'What work do you do?' I used to answer: 'Oh, I'm a writer'. Which is quite a lie because I've hardly written a thing, and I've tried but I know I just wouldn't be able to earn a living by writing. Working people are earning a living. I won't truthfully be a writer until I'm *earning* something from the business.

When they said: 'Oh, that's interesting and what have you written?' I would say: 'Well . . . I have two unpublished manuscripts. One got lost in the post. The other got lost among the papers and rubble on a publisher's desk.' Nobody believed me, of course, and funnily enough I was telling the truth. I didn't have the guts to defend myself because I wouldn't have liked them to read what I had written. It was a hotch-potch of under-done ideas, and monotonous in the extreme. There was always a Coloured man here, an African man there and a white somewhere around the corner. Always the same old pattern. I tried to be poetic but even that didn't help. I just bored myself to death and I assumed that I would bore others too so I shut my mouth pretty quick about what I had written. If I had to write one day I would just like to say *people is people* and not damn white, damn black. Perhaps if I was a good enough writer I could still write damn white, damn black and still make people *live*. Make them real. Make you love them, not because of the colour of their skin but because they are important as human beings.

For instance, I would like to write the story about a man who is a packing hand at the railways and lives in one of the tumbling down, leaky houses in District Six. One year for his annual leave he decided to make use of the railway concession and take a free train ride with his wife to Durban. All the neighbours knew

6

about it because they are a popular and sociable couple, as are most people in District Six. No one has much of a private life in District Six. The neighbours make it their business to know all about you and they don't mind what your sins are. In fact, if it comes to the push they'll defend even if the law considers you in the wrong. The only suspicious man in District Six is the man who doesn't show his face and keeps a closed door. We are the real good and jolly neighbours, minding each other's business the way neighbours should. We can't help it because we're all piled up on each other.

Well, to get back to the story. This man and his wife had a crowd of friends tagging along as they went to catch the train to Durban. Ticket and booking all arranged. Bags stacked with food for the journey. Things like roast fowl, fish cakes, meat balls and plenty of sandwiches and some booze. The wife, a huge, adventurous, generous, loud-talking, happy and care-free woman climbed on the train first. The husband remained on the platform with the friends. He was sort of glum with a I'm-figuring-this-thing-out look on his face. He always gets that look on his face when he's not too pleased about something. Just as the first warning bell rang he shouted with real terror in his voice: 'Ma, get off. Let's go home.' And that was that. He didn't even have to explain. Everyone understood. To leave Cape Town and go gallivanting around like some fool in a foreign place like Durban would be an act of the most vile treachery. Cape Town is his home. He was born here. He will die here. Besides, nobody in Durban would understand him. He has a very special kind of language. His very own. He has a special kind of face that is comfortingly reflected in the faces around him. Those faces swear with the exact same nuance that he does. They eat the exact same food. They have the exact same humour. Why go to that fool of a place called Durban? What is there in it for him? To leave Cape Town would be like dying. It would be the destruction of all that he is as a man. He just doesn't have the kind of pretentiousness that makes an American tourist come and gape at the Zulu dances.

Well there it is. I would like to write the story of the man and his wife who never took the train journey, but I can't. When I think of

7

writing any single thing I panic and go dead inside. Perhaps it's because I have my ear too keenly attuned to the political lumberjacks who are busy making capital on human lives. Perhaps I'm just having nightmares. Whatever my manifold disorders are, I hope to get them sorted out pretty soon, because *I've just got to tell a story*.

1962

An unspeakable crime

◆

There is something terribly sinister happening. Why are the Coloureds, with unashamed determination handing over the education of their children to the Coloured Affairs Department? In Port Elizabeth and Cape Town they are doing this terrible act with conviction and a maddening self compulsion. They are not forced. The infamous 'Bantoe-onderwyswet' was forced on the African people amidst vigorous protest. The Coloureds are running over each other to lend an ear to the government and its good boys, and, they are not one bit ashamed of what they are doing. I should clearly state, of course, that it is not all the Coloureds who are doing the talking. It is those few – the fat pompous principals and all the you-know-who. Those who have remained neutral and Pontius Pilates are also accessors to the crime.

Are the whole mass of Coloureds intentional supporters of this intolerable status quo? Have they ever had a chance? Have they been conditioned like dogs to accept whatever comes to them? Have they lived too long in abysmal poverty and hopelessness so that nothing matters anyway?

The average Coloured is a semi-literate or illiterate, inarticulate man trapped in a round of misery, poverty and week-end drunkenness; a timid God-fearing law abiding citizen of his own particular hell.

What hope is there for a child; a typical Coloured child who

8

starts life in a home like this? At the age of three months he is introduced to horrifying brutal violence. One morning his mother and father quarrel. There is no money and food in the home as the father has spent it on drink. As he walks out of the house the mother throws their three month old son into the street after him. It is unbelievable, but it is true.

Another woman has five illegitimate children whom she supports on char work; washing and ironing for 25c a day.

These two cases are not exceptions. They are almost the rule and can be re-counted in millions. It is also a well-known fact that the Coloureds are the greatest beggars in the land and practically live on the board-of-aid. Nothing alleviates the vicious circle of their misery. Just nothing.

These children need all the help that a truthful, normal education can give them; not an education that is going to grind them back into muck. But who cares about them? All that the 'negotiators' and 'liaison committees' are concerned about are the teachers' salaries. Fix that up and everything else is in the bag.

It is shocking to look on at the treachery of these men because they are selling out a people who do not know how to speak for themselves and who cannot seem to realize the magnitude of the crime that is being committed against them.

1963

A gentle people

◆

The warm, uncommitted 'Coloureds' of the Cape

When I first came to Cape Town in 1958, my friends told me that Cape Town would weave a spell around me and I should never be able to leave it. If I went away, they said, I would always come back. Their words have proved true. I have come back, again and again, not knowing what it is that draws me. Now I do know. I love the Cape because it can give me, a writer, a fierce individual-

9

ist – a warmth, a love, a sense of something that is the opposite of isolation and a sense of belonging, if not to the country, at least to the human race. I have found all this among the Coloured community in the Cape.

Whites in the Cape, with the habitual arrogance of whites, refer to the Cape as having a 'liberal tradition'; meaning of course, '*their* liberal tradition'. It would never occur to them that it is the basically gentle and unaggressive personality of the Cape Coloured that has made them 'liberal'. Wherever the white has felt himself 'threatened' he has never hesitated to clamour for the most ruthless army and police repression. He lives always with his fears. The fact that he is able to pride himself in the Cape on being 'liberal' is because he does not fear the Coloured man.

Another fallacy of the whites is that they are the preservers of White Western Christian culture in Africa. Culture is not limited to the West, or Europe or a white skin or Christianity. Culture, in its truest sense, in its universal sense is the expression of the *personality* of a people. The Cape Coloured has this personality and he expresses it in little gestures and habits that are unique and belong to him alone. In fact his sense of belonging to himself and understanding himself without desires to impose himself on others gives him a wonderful sense of a relaxed enjoyment of living. In a country where the rest of the oppressed groups are hounded day in and day out, their homes broken up, their movements restricted, he has been able to live in relative peace and move about as freely as he wished. To do this he achieved a compromise with the ruling, dominant group. Superficially he has many outward mannerisms and speech similarities of the Afrikaner. But the Afrikaner did not want him and yet did not fear him so he has developed from a bit here and a bit there a personality of his own. He adapts and grows and absorbs, adding to himself all the time. He welcomes strangers, is curious and interested in them and with a quick wit and jolly humour puts on a bit of their garments. He even adopts Hollywood and all its quaint trash. Anything and anyone can live beside him: sometimes these mixtures make him a better man, sometimes they have a harmful influence. In a cold and loveless country like South Africa his warmth of heart and

10

genuine friendliness is like a great roaring fire on the white icy wastes of the Antarctic.

◇

In spite of the advantages, such as freedom of movement that the Coloured man has had over the other oppressed groups in South Africa, he has, either through an innate laziness, lack of initiative or maybe even a sheer crazed honesty not made financial capital out of his advantages. He is on the whole perpetually poor, uncomplaining about his poverty and no trouble at all. On top of all that, he is that infuriating character – the uncommitted man. He has given his loyalty to *no one*. How can he when he cannot even agree with himself about what he is thinking?

The negative aspects of Cape Coloured leadership tend to stress the fact that the fate of the Cape Coloured people is the fate of the white in South Africa. If that were really true then the Coloured man is doomed. But it is not. The Coloured man knows he is oppressed, and he knows his oppressor. He of all oppressed groups in South Africa fears his oppressor most because he is closer to him and really understands the ruthless nature of his power. So, he complies. He is obsequious, just so long as everybody leaves him in peace. Instead he would rather expend his hidden rage and frustration in drink and acts of violence on his own people or else try to outwit and make fun of you with his shrewd sense of humour. Some Coloured leaders would appear to be unaware of the tragedy that is the day to day life of the Coloured people. They would give the impression that the Coloured man is working hand in glove with the oppressor. The real trouble with these leaders is that they have created a conservative middle class of their own which is but a pallid and watery reflection of white privilege. It is a treacherous, dangerous and deceiving reflection.

◇

The racialists in the South of the United States of America are making their last stand. The pro-tribalists are or will be making their last stand. We are told that the hard core of Afrikanerdom in South Africa will also make its last stand. A decisive factor for a man in all these strifes and last stands is for him for the sake of his self-respect to find out where his loyalty lies. A man who sees a country merely as a place where he can earn money is not loyal to that country; his loyalty lies some other place, and, as soon as he has collected enough will be agetting back to that place. Neither is a man loyal who values a country only for the privileged position he holds there. Colonialists dominated in Africa for so long only because there was no other force to counter their power. When they had to contend with the uncompromising force of African nationalism, they gave way; sometimes gracefully; sometimes with a fierce and bitter struggle.

There is often the cry of non-white leaders in this country, and among Coloured leaders in particular, about the lack of unity among the oppressed people. Leaders, especially some sinister and unscrupulous ones which we have here, wish to use the people for their own ends; for ends that may mean either a perpetuation of white domination or the introduction of something like Moscow rule. Africa and the awakened forces of African nationalism are against them and against all exploiters who do not admit a loyalty to a continent that has had its fill of exploitation. Future generations of young people in South Africa and Africa will be against them too.

We all love our comfortable grooves and somehow feel safe in patterns of living that have been imposed upon us; even though these patterns are unjust. A time of change is a time of upheaval that disrupts the status quo. It is also a time when violent passions rampage and terrifying acts of repression are perpetrated by those who wish to resist this change. The sane man will resist being swept into this cauldron of hatred. He learns to accept change as one of the inevitable consequences of life and prepares to adjust himself to something new, well knowing that the past was not good for him and looking forward with hope to the future.

Who knows what is ahead? But life has need of a people such as the Coloured people of the Cape. While they too are suffering at the hand of the exploiter and do not as yet know whether they are

12

this or that or here or there, they are warmly human, generous with a word of greeting and a smile. For my part, they evoke the words of Stephen Foster, later used in a popular song – 'dear hearts and gentle people.'

1963

Letter from South Africa

◆

For a friend, 'D.B.'

One is constantly losing friends these days. Some of the refugees, like my friend, 'D.B.' did not want to leave. Wherever he is now, I know he is very unhappy. For those of us who are still here, life becomes lonelier and intensely isolated. South Africa is an intensely lonely, intensely sad country. It must have always been but you only begin to notice the loneliness and sadness when all your friends are gone. Friendship is like the part of you that is not very brave; and, if you have friends you find yourself rising to extraordinary heights of strength. You get up to crazy schemes; you talk crazy and it is as though with your friends you will fix up all the wrongs in the world. Suddenly that happy, warm laughing world is shattered and you are left alone to face a horror too terrible to contemplate.

Of all countries in the world, South Africa is the one country where you need friends. True enough, the butcher will tell you everything is getting very bad. But he gets terrified if you comment on his statement. He doesn't want to interfere with the 'government'. It's like that with nearly everybody in your immediate vicinity. The best, the most sane people have left and you find yourself having to put up with slobs who tell you that the P.A.C. sabotaged Goldreich's plane in Bechuanaland!

With such a state of affairs you are bound to lose your sense of humour and I do not think that there is anything quite as painful as not being able to laugh; sometimes. For one thing an apathy

13

and a passiveness overcome you and you get into the dangerous
state of mind of being wrapped up in your own troubles and
miseries. You cannot think. You cannot live. It's just yourself all
the time. For another, a fatal feeling of doom pervades everything.
It is like those faces in pictures that you see of the people who had
to live in the Warsaw ghetto. They were finally forced to face the
fact that they had a ruthless and unrelenting enemy and help was
nowhere in sight. Every white face that you see passing by churns
you up till you could just cry to be delivered from this unceasing
torment of hate, hate, hate. You wonder if that fat, smug
complacent white matronly face was the one who wrote the letter
in last night's paper . . . 'We have people in our midst who have
just recently emerged from savagery . . .' She was complaining
about an advert in the paper for slimming pills which showed a
naked white woman on a scale. They still write these crazy letters.
Aren't they scared enough?

Maybe I am going to pieces. One of the slobs who are left
behind told me rather scornfully the other day that I was not a
freedom fighter. I have to admit that it is the truth. I never joined
fund-raising campaigns because I can't ask for money. I never
paid at fund-raising parties because I was always broke and yet
drank as much wine as I could and talked as loud as I could and
quarrelled with the whites who were there. The 'liberal' whites
seemed to like one to fight because they always provoked the
arguments as far as I was concerned and always laughed at
offensive remarks. Yes, maybe I am going to pieces because I was
never the type to rush around doing things. I just sat around
talking all the time and now all those beautiful ideas have blown
up in my face. You can't think straight about anything if you're
hating all the time. You even get scared to write because
everything has turned cock-eyed and sour. This would never have
happened if my friend 'D.B.' were around. He hated that kind of
mentality, and with his sarcastic wit and optimism would have
made me seem a complete fool. That is why you need friends like
that. They have something you lack, like optimism. They make
you feel everything is going to be all right with the world as long as

14

they are around. It may seem a childish thing to be so dependent on friends. But is it really?

The fantastic thing about friendships in South Africa is that one always and only meets one's friends through politics. Every and any man, woman who ever thinks in this country gravitates to some political party. Outside this you may have friends but none that you could carry on a reasonable or intelligent conversation with. Many people prefer not to be enlightened. The world terrifies them and yet their very refusal to be enlightened terrifies them more. They are vaguely aware that 'all is not right in the state of Denmark', they are constantly tugged this way and shattered by this so they flee to God to protect them from their fears. One can't help admiring political people. They never talk about God. I do not, of course, wish to imply that my political friends are non-believers like myself. It is just that we have been too busy arguing about George Padmore to have any time left over for such a subject.

Now they are all gone, those brave optimistic characters! One misses them furiously! One is left with all the believers and the slobs and the enemy. One longs for a place

'to give what's left of love again,
to friends, now strangers.'

1963

Gladys Mgudlandlu: the exuberant innocent

◆

The white-collared raven reposes with god-like indifference near a clump of bushes. The chief's wife, with a sharp glint of mischief in her shrewish eyes, puffing away fiercely at a corn pipe, listens to the latest gossip. The hot, orange velvet flowers; the deep green valleys; the hard brown sunbaked hills, and – the large crowd of eager admirers and eager buyers showering an astonishing and almost unbelievable adulation on the artist, Miss Gladys Mgud-

15

landlu. Since her last exhibition in Cape Town, which was a sweeping success, the crowd of admirers has doubled and trebled, so much so that almost four hundred of the eight hundred people who attended the opening of her exhibition this month could not gain admittance.

◇

What is the secret of the phenomenal success of Miss Mgudlandlu? Undoubtedly much of her work is strong. Each piece is a new, fresh idea. In fact new ideas seem to crowd in on her all the time and she appears to be in such haste to rush after the new burst of inspiration that one is left with the uneasy impression that each picture is slap-dash and incomplete. Compared to the clean-cut, sharp and brilliant technique of the Johannesburg artist, Ephraim Ngatane, Miss Mgudlandlu indulges in mere childish scrawl. It is interesting briefly to make a comparison between Mr. Ngatane and Miss Mgudlandlu. When he exhibited in Cape Town two months ago he received a dead-cold snub. He is an intense, passionate controlled, vividly imaginative artist and his Township Scenes rebound and vibrate with life. The trouble with Mr. Ngatane, it seems, is that his intensity and realistic approach is irksome. He reminds people, who would rather forget, that townships are nasty places where people have to walk some two hundred yards to fetch water from a communal tap shared by some 80,000 township's inhabitants. He is annoying too, because, behind the colour, the hysterical exhilaration of his massed and teeming streets, is the degradation of poverty. Who wants to be reminded of the terrors of township living? It is ugly, horrible and sordid. So, let the ambiguous Mr. Ngatane rot; the fate of all those who shatter the calm of society's built-in illusions.

Miss Mgudlandlu, on the other hand, performs a kindly service. She is an escapist. Her message is: 'Leave it all to God. God is in his heaven and all is right with South Africa.' In her calm green valleys through which half-naked tribal women wend their peace-ful way homeward in the late African sunset one can recline restfully with a cocktail and the past is the future and the present is the past while Miss Mgudlandlu soothingly murmurs: 'Come *Deep*

16

in the Forest. Gaze at the *Velvet Flowers*; the *Birds and Lilies*; the *Forest Rockery*; the *Hills and Dongas*; the *Precipice*; the *Migrant Birds*; the *Elephant Trunk* . . . Ah, . . . there's *No Life Without Religion*.' Who can resist her hypnotic call when life and reality mean ninety-day detentions and banning orders and bang, bang, bang? For a few seconds I could see the attraction in those cool dark clumps of trees and birds and lilies and elephant trunks! I too would care for a brief escape from the permanent madness of reality! And, I believe that it is on the appeal of this escape release that she so profusely and exuberantly provides, that Miss Mgudlandlu's phenomenal success rests. Miss Mgudlandlu is too innocent and unaware to have deliberately contrived this state of affairs. As an artist I believe her to be truthful within her capacities and limitations. There is simply a demand for escape and she is the unconscious supply. Had there not been this demand I for one do not believe that Miss Mgudlandlu would be basking in warmth of overwhelming public adulation. In fact, such sweeping, hysterical uncritical acclaim is disastrous for an artist who must always be subjected to those agonising doubts which spur him on to greater and higher achievements. It amused me to hear Miss Mgudlandlu continuously exclaim to visitors: 'This is my best picture. Why don't you buy it?'

1963

Snowball: a story

◆

It is autumn in Cape Town. Each day the sunset is new, with a new theme, but the underlying mood is always the same. Always the still, chilled autumn air controls the earth's scent with a nostalgic sweetness that is unlike any other season of the year. Sharp, and distinct, these scents blend with the yellow-gold sky as it imperceptibly changes to a powdery mauve and then a vivid,

17

splashy orange-red that pulsates and pulsates. Two children pass by, barefoot, absorbed, with comic red-painted sunset faces. Suddenly the sharp black silhouette of rooftops appear outlined against the glowing sky.

It is strange how a scene or a street can evoke pleasant or unpleasant memories. It is strange, too, how one's life is rather like a railway station. People pass in and out all the time and yet so few are of consequence to one's destiny. If the sunset reminds me of 'Snowball' it is only because during the time I knew him I was driven by a strong urge to protect him. He was too passive and peace-loving and life knocked him around an awful lot. He merely took each blow as it came without question or thought of retaliation. I imagine the only peace he ever found was when he was at sea in his small dinghy. I imagine, too, that he was the kind of man who would notice a sunset.

Capetonians have a witty way of giving people queer nick-names. But often these nicknames make sense. Just say all the fingers of one hand may be missing, then they might call you 'Vyf' and you would not mind at all because the way in which it was said would bear a tender regard for your defect; even to the point of giving you great prestige in the neighbourhood. But the nickname 'Snowball' never really made sense to me because 'Snowball' was a man who was quite black all over except for his clean white teeth. I must admit that there are many things in Cape Town that confuse me! Strangely enough 'Snowball' did not mind being called 'Snowball' though had I been in his place, I would have made every effort to acquire another nickname. It just would have made me hot all over to be called 'Snowball'.

I first met 'Snowball' when we moved into a crowded four-roomed house in District Six. The housing situation being what it is, my husband and I were immensely grateful to obtain a clean large room to ourselves with a bathroom and were prepared to put up with the hazardous and inexplicable behaviour of our landlord and landlady. Our landlord was forever threatening us with bodily assault, ably abetted by our landlady who alternately suffered from fits of wild generosity and wild anger. One never knew where one stood in such a storm-filled atmosphere. I myself am not usually very obliging. I loathe to be at the mercy of those who make irrational demands. But then life can teach one some very humbling lessons. If my landlady said: 'Put out the light,' I put it out. If, five minutes later she said: 'Put it on,' I put it on. But underneath the rebel fumed and fumed and frequently there were sharp explosions; threats of physical violence, a lot of hot air and an electric tension which were as suddenly stilled by an outburst of wild generosity on the part of my landlady. It always overcomes me when an enemy reaches out the hand of peace. I'm terribly bad at making up.

With my husband there was never a note of discord. He is naturally tactful and a skilful negotiator of human relationships. They adored him. All in all, we the tenants, were a subdued lot; 'Snowball' perhaps the most subdued of us all. I mean, we all had a little party now and then, took a drink and sort of let go. But 'Snowball' had forsaken all worldly pleasures. He was a convert and every evening one would see him quietly sitting in some obscure corner with his head stuck in the Bible. But it made no difference. It only goaded everyone, my landlady in particular, into reminding him loudly that he was once a professional thief and all those bruises and scars on his face were because he had served an eight-year jail sentence. To them, 'Snowball's' religion was a cover up. A thief is always a thief. It must have taken great strength of character to stick to religion in the face of such provocation.

It is important to expand a bit on Snowball's religion. It was very wide and broad-minded wherein science and spiritualism and all other contradictory ideas could live in chaotic happiness. I have immense respect for such broad-mindedness. It appears to me, from the way they talk, that many converted people severely restrict themselves to reading the Bible. Darwin is out, because he contradicts the story of Adam and Eve. Aldous Huxley is definitely out, because he once had the audacity to say that God was unnecessary. Well, before I ever came to discussing 'Snowball's' religion with him, I had a peek into his room, saw Aldous Huxley

19

and his 'Perennial Philosophy' among all those pamphlets, leaflets and paths of truth. It surely helps to introduce a lot of contradiction into religion. I think so.

The first question 'Snowball' asked me when we got to discussing things was whether I was a soul with a body or a body with a soul. Since I have many converted friends I was bound to know the answer to that one, so I answered promptly: 'I am a soul with a body.'

I was amazed at the smile of intense happiness that spread over his face. I felt like a cheat because it must have taken him and my friends many gruelling hours of thought to have arrived at any sort of answer that satisfied them. The question does not concern me either way but then I had to learn that my flippant, cynical attitude towards religion is useless. Possibly it was only a man like 'Snowball' who could give me a humbling lesson in that direction. For one thing, he was basically good and gentle. That is something that cannot be faked . . . goodness. For another, he had a curious mind that was incapable of taking a dogmatic stand. Contradiction or even apparent contradiction could be called the other name of truth. That night 'Snowball' and I discussed many things that are not even mentioned in the Bible.

I would have liked to be a strong ally and defend and protect 'Snowball' from all the harsh blows that landed on his head. An impossible task! Once I tried. I heard our landlady loudly berating him for being a dirty man. I could not see how he could be, because he was the only tenant in the house who bathed every night. I told her so, but she looked at me blankly, pretending not to hear. I never tried again. In fact, one just became accustomed to hear 'Snowball' getting it in the neck again about something or other. His crayfish had a way of lying dead for hours and then suddenly arising and walking about the house. He could hardly pay the rent because each day a well-to-do cousin seized three-quarters of the profits on the fish under the pretext that he had paid for the dinghy. Something was always happening to 'Snowball'.

One day, during a sudden high summer gale, his dinghy

capsized, and I have as yet found no answer to the people who pass in and out of my life.

The isolation of 'Boeta L.'

Atteridgeville in 1964

That single long stretch of road from Pretoria West: and then; the sharp left turn. Another brief blind view of gently rolling hills; and then; the first lonely, shattered, deserted outpost – the 'Watch-boys' office. From that point, hidden in a valley one can see the myriad doll-like houses of the township, Atteridgeville.

Possibly nothing can adequately describe the complete isolation of a community like Atteridgeville. To the eye of the stranger it is an island in itself and its people live and move with the close fellowship of an island community. One thought, one action can occur to many people at the same time. For instance, it is now a prevalent trend for mothers to 'fix' the hair of girl children from about the age of five upwards with a harsh chemical called 'cold-straight'. This fad may soon cease, however, as many children now have large bald patches on their heads. The chemical destroys the hair cells.

Another trend is for young girls to have babies outside mar-riage. In fact it is most difficult for the young to marry as most parents look upon their daughter's lovers as 'criminals'. The term 'criminal' may apply to anyone who won't work because he does not care to wake at four or five in the morning and journey some eight to thirty-six miles to a place of employment. If you have a job in Silverton you have to wake up at five as there is one early train at five-forty-five. The next train is many hours later. In winter, when it is dark in the early morning you lose your job because you are late for work. People are condemned to a far-flung area with hazardous transport. In this area there is no scope for business enterprise. The Municipality owns this and the Municipality owns that. So, the young girls accept their illegitimate babies and the unemployed young men become increasingly violent and restless in their frustration. People have learnt to live with frequent and brutal murders. No one moves a step to assist a voice crying for help in a dark street. It is incredible – this daily battle against fear, sudden violence and extreme poverty.

Politically, Atteridgeville strikes an outsider as rather cowardly. People say: 'Let the people of Lady Selborne do the fighting but please leave us alone. Lady Selborne is a powder keg but we are just big luggage. You can't move us.'

Then they laugh indulgently and add: 'You see what happened to the bus boycott? We did not want to walk. Everybody in Lady Selborne walked. Then the Government withdrew the buses in Atteridgeville so that it could give us a train service.'

Transport is awful. Most trains run hourly and are extremely congested. People working in Pretoria go in by taxi which costs them thirty cents a return trip. From a wage of R8 per week, very little is left over for household needs.

There was once a fierce political individualist in Atteridgeville called 'Boeta L'. He has now been converted to religion. Some people say he was converted to religion because he was sad and despairing that no one would support his cause. But the people argue that 'Boeta L.' was only acting for 'his own sweet self.' For instance, he never informed anyone that he was going to rush up to Dag Hammerskjold that day with a Bible and say: 'Take back your Bible, White Man. This is an eye blind. You tell us to go to church while you are in the battle-field!'

Afterwards everyone admonished him: 'Boeta, you must not do such things. They will put you in jail. Besides, Dag Hammerskjold did not invent the Bible.'

This is so typical of the tough, cynical humour of the people of Atteridgeville. They like to say that they are very good at following funerals but not so good at following politicians.

It is difficult to get a clear account of the shattered 'Watchboys'' office at the entrance to the Township. It might be Atteridgeville's one political action. A few years ago there used to be a 'Watchboy' and several police stationed at the office. All visitors or strange cars used to be stopped and a policeman would then climb into the car and accompany the occupants to wherever they wished to go. One night, the 'Watchboy' went out on a spree and the office was smashed good and thoroughly. Soon after, all 'Watchboys' and police were removed. The authorities said it was expensive to maintain. Today the 'Watchboys'' office is a curious and deserted outpost that cannot help but give one a twitch of amusement as one passes by.

1964

2

In Exile:

Botswana
1964–1979

Preface to 'Witchcraft'

I like a repetition of everyday events – the weather, the sunrise, or going to the same spot every day, depending on whether that spot is hallowed ground. I am most unhappy in unholy places. So, while knowing my ideal and the simplicity of my own needs, I have continually lived with a shattering sense of anxiety – that human beings are unfortunately set down in unholy places, and Southern Africa may be the unholiest place on earth.

Any biographical detail takes in innumerable people of my generation who are scattered throughout the world as refugees. We were forced out of South Africa because, unlike our parents and our ancestors, we refused to call the white man *baas* ('master'). In South Africa it was always the white man or woman we considered to be living at death's door, because we could kill them rather than cower . . . I think we are as desperate as anything to make Africa the black man's land because I see no other place on earth where the black man may come into his own, with dignity.

I have a sort of bitter ha, ha, ha behind everything I say. I knew some time ago that I am a useless kind of person in any liberation movement or revolution; I can't stand them or the people who organize them. But I did move, in 1964, one door away from South Africa to Botswana. Botswana became independent in 1966, with a government that turned out to have an extremely hostile policy toward South African refugees. In 1966 they put us on a police roll, and from then to this day I have been reporting to the police every week. A few refugees applied for Botswana citizenship and were turned down.

The thing about Botswana is that it is a vast, semi-desert, and drought-stricken land, and all through its history it attracted few white settlers. A bit of ancient Africa was left almost intact to dream along in its own way. In South Africa the white man took even the air away from us – it was his air and his birds and his land. In Botswana, I have a little bird outside my window every day. No one laid any particular claim to him, so I am able to confide, to the whole world, that he sings like this, and he sings like

27

that, without some white man or woman snickering behind my ear: 'Why, you people don't appreciate things like *that*!'

I once attended a multi-racial party in South Africa. I sat next to a white woman and chatted, and during the conversation I foolhardily mentioned that I had a crush on Albert Camus and thought he had the death wish. She immediately turned and twittered loudly to the whole company: 'Did you hear what Bessie said? She thinks Camus had the death wish.' It is a humiliation to even talk to such mediocre people.

The least I can ever say for myself is that I forcefully created for myself, under extremely hostile conditions, my ideal life. I took an obscure and almost unknown village in the Southern African bush and made it my own hallowed ground. Here, in the steadiness and peace of my own world, I could dream dreams a little ahead of the somewhat vicious clamour of revolution and the horrible stench of evil social systems. My work was always tentative because it was always so completely new: it created new worlds out of nothing; it battled with problems of food production in a tough semi-desert land; it brought all kinds of people, both literate and semi-literate together, and it did not really qualify who was who – everyone had a place in my world. But nothing can take away the fact that I have never had a country; not in South Africa or in Botswana where I now live as a stateless person.

1975

SKETCHES

□

Africa was never 'the dark continent' to African people . . .

from: *Serowe: Village of the Rain Wind* **1981**

For Serowe: a village in Africa

◆

Summertime in Serowe is an intensely beautiful experience. It rains unpredictably, fiercely, violently in November, December, January. Before the first rains fall it gets so hot that you cannot breathe. Then one day the sky just empties itself in a terrible downpour. The earth and sky heaves alive and there is magic everywhere. The sky takes on a majestic individuality and becomes a huge backdrop for the play of the rain. Not ordinary rain but very peculiar rain.

All through December and January the rain sways this way and that on the horizon. The wind rushes through it and you get swept about by a cold fresh rain-wind. Sometimes all the horizon rain sweeps across the village in glistening streams. Then the grass roofs of the mud huts shine like polished gold. The barren earth, grazed to a shred by the goats, becomes clothed by a thin fine carpet of green. Under the trees there is a sudden, lush wild growth of long green grass. Everything is alive in this short dazzling summer. Forgotten are the long months of bleaching scorching sun and intense blue skies. The sky is now shaded with large brooding clouds.

It takes such a long while for the insects to come out of hibernation. But in December the earth teems with them. There are swarms of flies, swarms of mosquitoes and swarms of moths –

29

sometimes as big as little birds. Crickets and frogs are all over in the pools and around the village; there is a heavy rich smell of breathing earth everywhere.

Somehow, by chance, I fled to this little village and stopped awhile. I have lived all my life in shattered little bits. Somehow, here, the shattered little bits began to come together. There is a sense of wovenness; of wholeness in life here. There were things I loved that began to grow on me like patches of cloth . . .

$\diamond$

There isn't anything in this village that an historian might care to write about. Dr. Livingstone passed this way, they might say. Historians do not write about people and how strange and beautiful they are – just living. There is so much necessity living they do and in this village there is so much mud living. Women's hands build and smooth mud huts and porches. Then the fierce November, December thunderstorms sweep away all the beautiful patterns. After some time these same patient hands, hard and rough, will build up these mud necessities again.

There are just people of Africa here and endless circles of mud huts. They do not seem to be in a particular confusion about anything. The politicians are very agitated because the whole of Southern Africa is a melting pot, they say. But the women just go on having babies and the families sit round the fire at night chatting in quiet tones. Everybody survives on little and there may be the tomorrow of nothing. It has been like this for ages and ages – this flat, depressed continuity of life; this strength of holding on and living with the barest necessities.

$\diamond$

They say this and that about aid. They seem to know nothing of the desperate longing to bring out our own creativeness. In Southern Africa this desperation is fierce because we feel that opportunities to venture out on discoveries of our own are going to be forcibly denied us for a long time. We are all really startled alive by the liberation of Africa, but we have been living in exclusive compartments for so long that we are all afraid of each other.

Southern Africa isn't like the rest of Africa and is never going to be. Here we are going to have to make an extreme effort to find a deep faith to help us to live together. In spite of what the politicians say people are not going to be destroyed. Not now. There is all this fierce hatred and it is real. There are the huge armies prepared for war against unarmed people and we are all overwhelmed with fear and <u>agony</u>, not knowing where it will end.

Some of us cannot battle with this conflict any more. I cannot. But wherever I go I shall leave a chunk of myself here because I think of myself as a woman of Southern Africa – not as a black woman but as an ordinary and <u>wryly</u> humble woman. There was this <u>immense</u> conflict, pressure, uncertainty and insecurity that I have lived with for so long. I have solved nothing. I am like everyone else – perplexed, bewildered and desperate.

1965

The woman from America

◆

This woman from America married a man of our village and left her country to come and live with him here. She <u>descended</u> on us like an avalanche. People are divided into two camps. Those who feel a fascinated love and those who fear a new thing. The terrible thing is that those who fear are always in the majority. This woman and her husband and children have to be sufficient to themselves because everything they do is not the way people here do it. Most terrible of all is the fact that they really love each other and the husband effortlessly and naturally keeps his eyes on his wife alone. In this achievement he is seventy years ahead of all the men here.

We are such a lot of <u>queer</u> people in the Southern part of Africa. We have felt all forms of suppression and are <u>subdued</u>. We lack the vitality, the push, the devil-may-care temperament of the people of the north of Africa. Life has to seep down to us from there and that pattern is already establishing itself. They do things first, then we. We are always going to be confederators and not initiators. We are very materialistically minded and I think this adds to our fear. People who hoard little bits of things cannot throw out and expand, and, in doing so, keep in circulation a flowing current of wealth. Basically, we are mean, selfish. We eat each other all the time and God help poor Botswana at the bottom.

Then, into this narrow, constricted world came the woman from America like an avalanche upon us. Some people keep hoping she will go away one day, but already her big strong stride has worn the pathways of the village flat. She is everywhere about because she is a woman, resolved and unshakeable in herself. To make matters worse or more disturbing she comes from the West side of America, somewhere near California. I gather from her conversation that people from the West are stranger than most people, and California is a place where odd and weird cults spring up every day. For instance, she once told me about the Church-of-the-Headless-Chicken! It seems an old woman bought a chicken but the place where she bought it was very haphazard about killing and plucking fowls. They did not sever the head properly and when the old woman brought the chicken home and placed it on the kitchen table, it sprang up out of the newspaper and began walking about with no head and no feathers – quite naked. It seems then that the old woman saw a vision, grabbed the chicken and ran next door to a neighbour who had been bed-ridden for many years, and, in great excitement, told him the strange happening. The poor old bed-ridden neighbour leapt from the bed, healed of his ailment and a miracle had been performed. The story spread like wild-fire and in a matter of hours money was collected, a congregation formed and the Church-of-the-Headless-Chicken was born. The chicken was interviewed by many newspapers and kept alive for some months on soluble food mixture dropped into its open gullet!

Then, another thing too. People of the West of America must be the most oddly beautiful people in the world; at least this woman from the West is the most oddly beautiful person I have ever seen. Every cross current of the earth seems to have stopped in her and blended into an amazing harmony. She has a big dash of Africa, a

32

dash of Germany, some Cherokee and heaven knows what else. Her feet are big and her body is as tall and straight and strong as a mountain tree. Her neck curves up high and her thick black hair cascades down her back like a wild and tormented stream. I cannot understand her eyes though, except that they are big, black and startled like those of a wild free buck racing against the wind. Often they cloud over with a deep, intense brooding look.

It took a great deal of courage to become friends with a woman like that. Like everyone here I am timid and subdued. Authority, everything can subdue me; not because I like it that way but because authority carries the weight of an age pressing down on life. It is terrible then to associate with a person who can shout authority down. Her shouting matches with authority is the terror and sensation of the village. It has come down to this. Either the woman is unreasonable or authority is unreasonable, and everyone in his heart would like to admit that authority is unreasonable. In reality, the rule is: If authority does not like you then you are the outcast and humanity associates with you at their peril. So, try always to be on the right side of authority, for the sake of peace, and please avoid the outcast. I do not say it will be like this forever. The whole world is crashing and inter-changing itself and even remote bush villages in Africa are not to be left out!

It was inevitable though that this woman and I should be friends. I have an overwhelming curiosity that I cannot keep within bounds. I passed by the house for almost a month, but one cannot crash in on people. Then one day, a dog they have had puppies and my small son chased one of the puppies into the yard and I chased after him. Then one of the puppies became his and there had to be discussions about the puppy, the desert heat and the state of the world, and as a result of curiosity an avalanche of wealth has descended on my life. My small hut-house is full of short notes written in a wide sprawling hand. I have kept them all because they are a statement of human generosity and the wide care-free laugh of a woman who is as busy as women the world over about things women always entangle themselves in – a man, children, a home . . . Like this . . .

'Have you an onion to spare? It's very quiet here this morning

33

and I'm all fagged out from sweeping and cleaning the yard, shaking blankets, cooking, fetching water, bathing children, and there's still the floor inside to sweep, and dishes to wash and myself to bathe – it's endless!'

Or again . . .

'Have you an extra onion to give me until tomorrow? If so, I'd appreciate it. I'm trying to do something with these awful beans and I've run out of all of my seasonings and spices. A neighbour brought us some spinach last night so we're in the green. I've got dirty clothes galore to wash and iron today.'

Or . . .

'I'm sending the kids over to get 10 minutes' peace in which to restore my equilibrium. It looks as if rain is threatening. Please send them back immediately so they won't get caught out in it. Any fiction at your house? I could use some light diversion.'

Or . . .

'I am only returning this tin in order to get these young folk out of my hair long enough pour faire my toilette. I've still cleaning up to do and I'm trying to collect my thoughts in preparation for the day's work. It looks like we face another scorcher today!'

And, very typical . . .

'This has been a very hectic morning! First, I was rushing to finish a few letters to send to you to post for me. Then it began to sprinkle slightly and I remembered you have no raincoat, so I decided to dash over there myself with the letters and the post key. At the very moment I was stepping out of the door, in stepped someone and that solved the letter posting problem, but I still don't know whether there is any mail for me. I've lost my P.O. Box key! Did the children perhaps drop it out of that purse when they were playing with it at your house yesterday?'

Or my son keeps getting every kind of chest ailment and I prefer to decide it's the worst . . .

'What's this about whooping cough! Who diagnosed it? Didn't you say he had all his shots and vaccinations? The D.P.T. doesn't require a booster until after he's five years old. Diphtheria – Pertussis (Whooping cough) – Tetanus is one of the most reliable vaccinations. This sounds incredible! You know all three of mine and I have had hoarse, dry coughs but certainly it wasn't whooping cough. Here's Dr Spock to reassure you!'

Sometimes too, conversations get all tangled up and the African night creeps all about and the candles are not lit and the conversation gets more entangled, intense; and the children fall asleep on the floor dazed by it all. The next day I get a book flung at me with vigorous exasperation . . .

'Here's C. P. Snow. Read him, dammit!! And dispel a bit of that fog in thy cranium. The chapters on Intellectuals and the Scientific Revolution are stimulating. Read it, dammit!!'

I am dazed too by Mr C. P. Snow. Where do I begin to understand the industrial use of electronics, atomic energy, automation in a world of mud huts? What is a machine tool? he asks. What are the Two Cultures and the Scientific Revolution? The argument could be quaint to one who hasn't even one leg of culture to stand on. But it isn't really, because even a bush village in Africa begins to feel the tug and pull of the spider-web of life. Would Mr Snow or someone please write me an explanation of what a machine tool is? I'd like to know. My address is: Serowe, Botswana, Africa.

The trouble with the woman from America is that people would rather hold off, sensing her world to be shockingly apart from theirs. But she is a new kind of American or even maybe will be a new kind of African. There isn't anyone here who does not admire her. To come from a world of chicken, hamburgers, T.V., escalators and what not to a village mud hut and a life so tough, where the most you can afford to eat is ground millet and boiled meat? Sometimes you cannot afford to eat at all. Always you have to trudge miles for a bucket of water and carry it home on your head. And to do all this with loud, ringing, sprawling laughter?

Black people in America care about Africa and she has come here on her own as an expression of that love and concern. Through her too, one is filled with wonder for a country that breeds individuals about whom, without and within, rushes the wind of freedom. I have to make myself clear, though. She is a different person who has taken by force what America will not give black people. We had some here a while ago, sent out by the State

Department. They were very jolly and sociable, but for the most innocent questions they kept saying: 'We can't talk about the government. That's politics. We can't talk politics.' Why did they come here if they were so afraid of what the American government thinks about what they might think or say in Africa? Why were they so afraid? Africa is not alive for them. It seems a waste of State Department's money. It seems so strange a thing to send people on goodwill projects and at the same time those people are so afraid that they jump at the slightest shadow. Why are they so afraid of the government of America which is a government of freedom and democracy? Here we are all afraid of authority and we never pretend anything else. Black people who are sent here by the State Department are tied up in some deep and shameful hypocrisy. It is a terrible pity because such things are destructive to them and hurtful to us.

The woman from America loves both Africa and America, independently. She can take what she wants from both and say: 'Dammit'. It is a most strenuous and difficult thing to do.

1966

Chibuku beer and independence

The rumour went about that Rhodesia was sending tankloads of free Chibuku beer for the Independence celebrations. To taste Chibuku beer again was almost like news from home for six young students and refugees in Francistown. They had fled from the university during the upheavals and detentions that accompanied UDI. They were eager to attend the celebrations and I went along too with my water bucket. The whole afternoon it was continuously over-flowing with Chibuku beer. We formed a tight circle in a shed and were as nasty as possible to strangers who begged a drink. Everyone had pretty pink plastic throw-away mugs and at the beer tank the law of the jungle prevailed, the

36

stronger shoving the weaker. We prided ourselves that we drank in peace and comfort.

There was just a raggle-taggle crowd of poor people wandering about aimlessly and uncertainly.

'They call this Independence,' one of the students said scornfully. 'Where's the excitement? Where's the fever?'

There were a lot more disparaging remarks.

'You should have been here at midnight,' someone said. 'The British flag was lowered in dead silence. Only one voice said hooray and everyone turned around to stare at the man in surprise. I was so furious I shouted: "burn it." Can you imagine my amazement? An old man standing next to me said I should not say such things. He said I am embarrassing everyone, especially the white people present.'

Everyone laughed because the people of Botswana really baffled them. It's as though you are thoroughly astonished to find yourself at the dead calm centre of a storm that rages over the whole of Southern Africa. You never quite get used to it if you have fled the whole night and day through wild country expecting at any moment to feel a police bullet whistling through your back. And the students had that air about them – keyed-up, wild, excitable, feverish. They burst out singing the sad, defiant anthem of Southern Africa and raised their hands to the Botswana flag. 'Africa is Ours,' they sang. And they kept repeating the anthem for half an hour. This drew a fascinated crowd that stood around silently, inspecting us minutely as though we were zoo animals.

We also sang:

'How many years does it take for a man to be free? –
. . . The answer is blowing in the wind . . .'

This depressed everyone and we sat in glum silence a few moments. An old man was sitting nearby. He had a perpetual smile on his wizened old face. He had walked many miles from the bush to celebrate independence. The skin on his knees was deeply creased and abnormally stretched from having spent most of his life in a squatting position. He looked at us with his beautiful smile and said in a touching childlike way: 'I like Francistown.'

37

Oddly, this aroused the students from their depression. They started to abuse everyone and everything again.

'You're drunk old papa,' they said.

'Who, just who in this silly country knows what independence means? Just ask anyone of these silly people.'

'Just look at that plain, ugly flag . . .'

'No, no,' I cut in sharply, suddenly aroused too. 'The flag is very beautiful. For one thing it is a flag for everyone, above party politics. For another it is truly symbolic of the country. One broad blue stripe represents the blue sky of Botswana, the other; the people's hope for rain to develop industry and agriculture. The black and white stripes, represent the ideal of racial harmony.'

They were a trifle disconcerted and looked at the flag again.

'All right,' someone said. 'I only like it when it's not blowing out full in the wind. I just like that broad stripe of black in the middle.'

Someone said something about the demerits of Seretse as an African politician. Then looked at me for I have lived in Botswana for almost three years.

'There's nothing wrong with the man,' I said mildly.

'What do you mean? Give us facts. Is he really an African nationalist?' they asked critically, unbelievingly.

I felt desperately uncomfortable being a non-supporter of politicians.

'He says sensible things,' I said, helplessly. 'I mean, the government is quiet and when it says something one examines it closely to see if there is any evil in the statement but you can't find it. You think perhaps it might be sensible then.'

'But is the man an African nationalist?' they asked.

'Yes,' I said. 'After a time I summed him up that way.'

Someone said: 'Actually, I can agree with her. I like a quiet man who shuts his mouth up when faced with a hopeless situation. Seretse is a much better politician than Dr. Banda of Malawi for instance. That man makes statements all the time and they are often detrimental to African interests.'

Our party broke up in a sudden, shocking and hilarious manner. We sent one of the students, a quiet, timid fellow to re-fill the bucket at the beer tank. Just as it was full he looked up into the sharp edge of a knife.

'Give it,' a drunken voice commanded. He hastily surrendered the bucket. Then the whole drunken crew of men about the tank fell upon the bucket with wild abandon and pulled it from end to end bathing their heads in beer. This was too much for the students. They flew into the fray, their arms in the air like wild birds. A Botswana policeman calmly intervened and tippled the remaining contents of the beer on the ground. The students ground their teeth in frustrated fury.

'These Batswana police are silly,' they said. 'We could have made a coup on that bucket without any bloodshed.'

I walked home alone. There was the ever-familiar thorn bush lit up by the brilliant fierce beauty of a desert sunset. Only a new unfamiliar feature; the blue, black and white flag straining in the strong breeze.

'It is all right,' I thought. 'The whole world seems topsy-turvy but there is a something here in this country that is good. Perhaps it is a weird kind of people who pull against the current; unprovokable; ever reasonable. Perhaps it is the rags and tatters of poverty that are worn with an upright posture and pathetic dignity. Whatever it is I say it is good because you feel it in your heart as peace.'

1966

Village people

◆

Poverty has a home in Africa – like a quiet second skin. It may be the only place on earth where it is worn with an unconscious dignity. People do not look down at your shoes which are caked with years of mud and split so that the toes stick out. They look straight and deeply into your eyes to see if you are friend or foe. That is all that matters. To some extent I think that this eye-looking, this intense human awareness, is a reflection of the earth

39

all about. There is no end to African sky and to African land. One might say that in its vastness is a certain kind of watchfulness that strips man down to his simplest form. If that is not so, then there must be some other, unfathomable reason for the immense humanity and the extreme gentleness of the people of my village.

Poverty here has majority backing. Our lives are completely adapted to it. Each day we eat a porridge of millet in the morning; a thicker millet porridge with a piece of boiled meat at midday; and at evening we repeat breakfast. We use our heads to transport almost everything: water from miles and miles, bags of corn and maize, and fire wood.

This adaptation to difficult conditions in a permanently drought-stricken country is full of calamity. Babies die most easily of starvation and malnutrition; and yet, within this pattern of adaptation people crowd in about the mother and sit, sit in heavy silence, absorbing the pain, till, to the mother, it is only a dim, dull ache folded into the stream of life. It is not right. There is a terrible mindlessness about it. But what alternative? To step out of this mindless safety, and face the pain of life alone when the balance is heavily weighted down on one side, is for certain to face a fate far worse. Those few who have, are insane in a strange, quiet, harmless way; walking all about the village, freely. Only by their ceaseless muttering and half-clothed bodies are they distinguishable from others. It is not right, as it is negative merely to strive for existence. There must be other ingredients boiling in the pot. Yet how? We are in the middle of nowhere. Most communication is by oxcart or sledge. Poverty also creates strong currents of fear and anxiety. We are not outgoing. We tend to push aside all new intrusions. We live and survive by making as few demands as possible. Yet, under the deceptive peace around us we are more easily confused and torn apart than those with the capacity to take in their stride the width and the reach of new horizons.

Do we really retain the right to develop slowly, admitting change only in so far as it keeps pace with our limitations, or does change descend upon us as a calamity? I merely ask this because, anonymous as we are, in our favour is a great credit balance of love and warmth that the Gods somewhere should count up. It may be that they overlook desert and semi-desert places. I should like to remind them that there are people here too who need taking care of.

1967

The old woman

She was so frail that her whole body swayed this way and that like a thin stalk of corn in the wind. Her arms were as flat as boards. The flesh hung loosely, and her hands which clutched the walking stick were turned outwards and knobbled with age. Under her long dress also swayed the tattered edges of several petticoats. The ends of two bony stick-legs peeped out. She had on a pair of sand-shoes. The toes were all sticking out, so that the feet flapped about in them. She wore each shoe on the wrong foot, so that it made the heart turn over with amusement.

Yet she seemed so strong that it was a shock when she suddenly bent double, retched and coughed emptily, and crumbled to the ground like a quiet sigh.

'What is it, Mmm? What is the matter?' I asked.

'Water, water,' she said faintly.

'Wait a minute. I shall ask at this hut here if there is any water.'

When I came back with the water, a small crowd had gathered.

'What is the matter?' they asked.

'The old lady is ill,' I said.

'No', she said curtly. 'I am not ill. I am hungry.'

The crowd laughed in embarrassment that she should display her need so nakedly. They turned away; but old ladies have no more shame left. They are like children. They give way to weakness and cry openly when they are hungry.

'Never mind,' I said, 'hunger is a terrible thing. My hut is not far away. This small child will take you. Wait till I come back, then I shall prepare food for you.'

Then, it was late afternoon. The old lady had long passed from

41

my mind when a strange young woman, unknown to me, walked into the yard with a pail of water on her head. She set it down outside the door and squatted low.

'Good-day. How are you?' I said.

She returned the greeting, keeping her face empty and carefully averted. It is impossible to say: what do you want? Whom are you looking for? It is impossible to say this to a carefully averted face and a body that squats quietly, patiently. I looked at the sky, helplessly. I looked at the trees. I looked at the ground, but the young woman said nothing. I did not know her, inside or out. Many people I do not know who know me, inside and out, and always it is this way, this silence.

A curious neighbour looked over the hedge.

'What's the matter?' she asked.

I turned my eyes to the sky again, shrugging helplessly.

'Please ask the young woman what she wants, whom she is looking for.'

The young woman turned her face to the neighbour, still keeping it averted, and said quietly:

'No, tell her she helped our relative who collapsed this morning. Tell her the relatives discussed the matter. Tell her we had nothing to give in return, only that one relative said she passes by every day on her way to the water tap. Then we decided to give a pail of water. It is all we have.'

Tell them too. Tell them how natural, sensible, normal is human kindness. Tell them, those who judge my country, Africa, by gain and greed, that the gods walk about her barefoot with no ermine and gold-studded cloaks.

1967

ESSAYS

□

Dear Sir,

I am enclosing a subscription slip. To me, at least, Transition *is
a kind of home. It seems to be fighting neither for communism or
capitalism. I am rather out of things and slick slogans and I do not
feel, as a communist has to, that I could have all the solutions to end
starvation and fix the world right – nor as a capitalist, who feels
pretty wonderful and secure with a million dollars . . .*

*We don't want to feel so driven and at the mercy of politicians.
We who want to be writers just cannot let the politicians subdue us
so. Politics (today) seems to have nothing to do with anyone and yet
is powerful enough to destroy human life. I really do not despair for
the future. It seems as though world-wide awareness of struggle and
suffering cannot help but lead to a sense of idealism in those who
rule. We cannot go back to the dark ages.*

Sincerely,
BESSIE HEAD

*Serowe
Bechuanaland*

Letter to Transition **1964**

God and the underdog

◆

Thoughts on the rise of Africa

There must be many people like me who first turn to the cartoon
quip page of the newspaper, but like me also, they must be

afflicted by a poor memory and forget the jokes the moment they have read them. Highly enshrined in the memory then are the one or two jokes one is destined never to forget. One of them goes like this: Two members of the Ku Klux Klan, named Clem and Jeff, were killed in a car at a railway crossing. Clem's soul reached heaven first, to be followed half an hour later by Jeff's. As Jeff reached the heavenly gates he saw Clem standing outside, looking white and shaken. Clem said to Jeff: 'Better watch your step, Jeff. I've just seen God and she's a Nigra.'

There were a few details left out. The 'Nigra' Goddess had looked at Clem with red eyes out of which poured all the fire and thunder and damnation of the Revelation and Clem had shuddered to the depths of his soul, not knowing what to expect next. Poor Clem. His civilisation had only prepared him for a salivating Jesus Christ with wishy-washy blue eyes whom he could make a walk-over on with the same cocksure bastardry as he had done on earth. For, in his heart of hearts, he deeply despised the King of the Jews. If he had not there would have been something to stop him from taking the body of living human beings, drenching them in hot tar, decorating them with feathers and setting them alight from the branch of a poplar tree. And he had done this laughing. And after he had roared away in his high-powered car there was only the charred body swaying and swaying in the star-bound breeze. And there was only the God of All Men observing this in silence. This is always his major trump card, this silence. It seems as though only the mystics and prophets have ever approached near enough to observe the nature of this terrible God. And how often have they given a description of the terror they saw to the unheeding human race . . .

'. . . That which is double-edged, that which is made of fire, that which is eternally alive. And he sendeth forth his word, straight and unswervingly, throughout all things . . .' And what is this word? . . . 'I have forbidden that men should commit iniquity, but their hearts have undone what my word decreed . . .'

Since in some part of my heart I bow down to the King of the Jews, it is impossible for me to blame the iniquity of the Ku Klux Klan on him, even though they painted him with blue eyes like one of their members. I set him apart from all this and accept him only as That which is double-edged, That which is made of fire. To me the white man is just the white man. And God is God. Perhaps I am only sorry that of all civilisations which have dominated this earth his has been the one most separated from God. For a long while I puzzled about this until one day I was accidently given the clue by a British volunteer.

This volunteer and I had been having an amiable discussion about the establishment of the State of Israel and during the discussion I happened to remark: 'There is nothing that moves me more deeply than the History of the Jews. They of all people have experienced most deeply and profoundly that God is the real Owner of the Universe . . .'

Being caught up in this thought, I was quite taken aback when the volunteer turned on me irritably and said: 'I don't like the way you say God is the Owner of the Universe.'

The first thing that occurred to me after this remark was only to walk away as quickly as possible. Because I was enraged. Because I wanted to say something like this: 'Do you think your bloody motor-car is the Owner of the Universe? Do you think a pip-squeak jiggling little white man like you is God? Why, you could drop dead this very minute.'

But I did not say this because I seemed to be labouring in some awful nightmare. I thought I hated the white man enough and I thought, through some queer logic, that I ought to love him through the volunteer because he is a better type of white man and also because he is in Africa helping with African development. The truth for me, at any rate, is that some of the volunteers brought me around to accepting the fact that the white man is human and perhaps one of them I admired without reserve because I sat with him in a hut of an old Batswana man. This volunteer was a Cambridge graduate and the old Batswana man said to him: 'I think the Good God does not like all the bad things in the world.' This had a profoundly moving effect on the Cambridge graduate. He even absent-mindedly drank a cup of tea into which several flies had fallen. It was really this volunteer, who was so deeply moved by a vision of God through an old Batswana

45

man, that for some time made me extremely enthusiastic about voluntary help quite out of touch with reality. It's there. Some of it is good. But Africa is going to rise to a great height of civilisation and this is going to be done, in the last resort, with African brains and my 'Nigra' Goddess.

I just accept it that my 'Nigra' Goddess is alive and real because I have nowhere else to turn for my salvation. I am one African who needs and wants my God Black, preferably 'Nigra' as Clem said she was and preferably of the feminine gender. There's something wrong with God, expressed as masculine. You don't see the fire and thunder in him the way you do in his feminine counterpart.

And if I say – My God, she's a 'Nigra' it is because I slightly confuse in my mind That which is double-edged, That which is made of fire, That which is eternally alive, with the personality of a certain Afro-American woman who was my friend and comrade for a period of almost two years in Botswana. It seems to me that I shall never forget her big, flashing, black eyes and her universal compassion for the Sudras or underdogs of the world. It seems to me that it is only the Afro-American, because of what they have suffered, who is capable of this deep compassion. Because when I compare her against us I really see the African continent as if filled with a lot of squabbling, petty-minded, vicious little tribalists who are likely, as in the case of Nigeria, to repeat the petty little bigotry of the tribal wars all over again, until the Gods, being fed up with this nonsense, send in some other colonial power to divide the continent of Africa up again for their own ends.

It has often amazed me how people substitute slushy emotions for such great words like friendship, compassion. You might feel soft and mushy about a little doggie. But between two living human beings there is always Truth and Truth is like that double-edged thing and is constantly expressing itself as Fireworks. Because when I look back on that friendship with the Afro-American woman I am often filled with hot resentment at the battering and bashing she gave me. I always seemed to have my mouth open and she always seemed to be bashing something down it. After all, I am one of the Sudras and she was a One-Eyed Jack with her fiery eye directed not only at the white man but the caste-ridden upper classes of India, or for that matter any oppressor of man. And they were all tabbed for the horrific judgement day. But in the meanwhile, I the Sudra, for whom she was supposed to feel compassion was treated in the most rough way.

Perhaps what made the friendship so painful and quarrelsome was that, at the time I'd met her I was going through some mental ditherings of my own. I had also just been relieved of the sight of the Afrikaner Boer and was correspondingly anxious to fill the great, empty, peaceful chambers of my heart with something beautiful like a God who was just quiet and full of common sense. Since these longings dominated my mind just then I'd often mention them wistfully during the brief pauses when my mouth wasn't open and something being bashed down it. I think that's why she said all those things to me — that I wasn't a genuine African, that I only longed to eat good food and that I might accidentally find myself with the damned on the judgement day. Because who was going to feed the poor while I communicated peacefully with my God? But after a time I began to take it because I thought I had the edge on her. I might not be a genuine African as she said. But I am most certainly a genuine Sudra because for the greater part of my life I only lived in the slums of South Africa where I was born. And from the way my friend walked and talked, she was like some upper-class American. She never swore. She never drank. While I did all this and worse in my life time. I also saw that we differed on the idea of violence. It's a small matter to me, when instantly enraged, to instantly kill someone stone dead, on the spot. And then all hell and heaven could kill me and I'd just laugh. Because that's my environment. It happened every day in front of my eyes when I was a child. On the other hand, my friend only saw violence in theory, as a vast social instrument for the judgement day. I don't think she knew what tricky material I really am. There's nothing neat and tidy about me, like a nice social revolution. With me goes a mad, passionate, insane, screaming world of ten thousand devils and the man or God who lifts the lid off this suppressed world does so at his peril.

It has already happened in all sorts of places in the world where my fellow brethen and Sudras were oppressed. It happened when

47

the Czars and Chinese landlords were torn to pieces. And it's still going to happen in India and Southern Africa. It seems as though the white man in Southern Africa is actually driving us towards it because his laws become harsher and harsher every day. And he won't pull out before it's too late.

Because what is not too late is the firm and established conviction that the underdog is already outside that closed door in which he was locked up. It is the most peculiar sensation and I can only express it in a personal way, restricted to the feelings of my own life. It was as though up to my generation we were all locked up together in a dark air-tight room. We even seemed to excrete together there and the stench was awful. Then some mysterious hand opened one of the windows and we received our first breath of fresh air which contrasted strongly with the stench in which we lived. At the same time this mysterious hand opened the door. And as we ran out we kept on saying: 'I'm not going back in there. I'm not going back in there.' A few of our oppressors who had been so accustomed to seeing us locked up, ran after us to put us back and we turned around and rent them to pieces. But we still have this sensation of running because of the horror out of which we have come. We don't know where we are running to except that we must run. Once I began to feel this sensation of running, running, it was at this point that I wanted a haven to run towards. Something that made sense. Something worthy of all the anguish of my life, because I can't have it mucked up by the politicians, by the tom-tom drum-beaters and crooks of our so-called liberatory organisations.

It's the way I feel about the revolutions of the world. When George Padmore told us to abhor Communism and choose the road of Pan Africanism, he only meant that the politicians in Russia were mucking up the show. He did not mean that his fellow brethren there were not right in ridding themselves of the Czars but that their anguish and suffering were being undermined by crooks. And there was such a passionate and torrential confusion in this revolution because no one seems to understand the underdog as he really is – that he is a passionate person without any nice, fancy manners. He is even more. He can be revolting.

48

Perhaps he and I are only this way because of the conditions in which we have lived for centuries and centuries. But we have to come out now. And perhaps we alone know how we will usher in this new age of universal brotherly love. For while we have as intense a capacity to destroy, so do we have as intense a capacity to build up, to create. Perhaps we won't be as selfish as the former rulers of the world. But our code has still to be written. Just as a side thought to this. It is interesting to note, that with the rise of the underdog has come out of it these philosophies of non-violence. Perhaps the creators of these philosophies unconsciously sense the damage and havoc we can really create, at any given moment.

Although I have said that there was this vast environmental difference between my American friend and I, it was really from her that I absorbed a capacity as an underdog to identify myself with all peoples in the world living under such conditions. It was her fiery eye fixed on Clem and Co. that made me see after all that God is not so silent as he is made out to be. The trouble is I don't know where my Goddess is just right now but there's certain things I'd like her to know about Clem and Co. and the conclusions I've drawn about him. I feel he's too mediocre for the gaze of her beautiful eyes and that she should just let him be and get the hell out of there back to Africa, some day.

Over and above us all is 'That which is double-edged, That which is made of fire, That which is eternally alive. And he sendeth forth his word, straight and unswervingly, throughout all things . . .' It is this thing which the white man is mocking, not the skin of the black man, for it is this thing, this terrific power which also created the black man. It's up to that power to do something about it. Clem didn't know what was coming next when he came face to face with his maker whom he had strung up, tarred and feathered and burnt to death on the poplar tree. But one thing I do know, that all this suffering has made Afro-American people catch a little of this fire from heaven and bring it down to earth to us. I wish with all my heart that they bring it to Africa because there are too few of us here, capable of catching this fire. It may be that all the ancient pharaohs and queens of our ancient civilisations have been born there and if they don't come back we will only be

49

left with our petty tribal wars and petty tribal customs. It seems as though we don't really have those large hearts and large eyes of the Gods. For largeness of heart is what we need for a civilisation and big, big eyes, wide enough to drink in all the knowledge of the heavens and earth. Why should people like this, like my Goddess, beg the white man for the crumbs that fall from his table? For that's what civil rights amount to. And they are so cynical about it, the giving of these crumbs.

The white man is not going to dominate us for many more years in Southern Africa. In the days of Egypt, before Joseph took his ten tribes there, there lived a pharaoh of whom it was written:

> 'The waters nourished him. All the birds of the air made their nests in his boughs, and all the beasts of the field brought forth their young under his branches. Beneath his shadow dwelt all the great nations. He was most beautiful in his greatness, because of the length of his roots, for his roots bathed in great waters . . .'

I feel in my heart that our Pharaoh has already been born. It may be that I shall not live to see Pharaoh's day but I want all those who now live in anguish to be comforted. For one day, due to the length of his roots and the depth of his wisdom, all nations shall dwell under his shadow.

1968

African religions
◆

Something repels the heart deeply in most organised forms of religion. There was a geography book of my school days with most of Asia blanked out as barbaric because Asians were so difficult to convert to Christianity. And there was a picture of a group of Untouchables standing by the sea-side and praying to the God, Shiva, the only God they were allowed to have because he never wanted much from mankind except a little water and Bel flowers. The caption under the picture said that the Untouchables were afraid to enter the temples, even though Indian law now allows them to do so.

Because we could not enter a place where gold ornaments were kept and incense burned in intricate rituals, we were discounted as a people having anything of value, as though our lives were a blanket of darkness or nothingness. You feel the agony of it in this age when we are supposed to borrow development and borrow everything either from Russia or America. Professor Mbiti, in his quiet and detached interpretations of African religions,[1] side-steps the snobs and explains the way of life of a mass of people who were for so long discounted in the scheme of things. Although he speaks of African people, the appeal his ideas have for me is that they are wide and generous enough to take in all the humble who shall, one day, unexpectedly, inherit the earth. It is hard to imagine a heaven where the Pope officiates, because so many people would have to be excluded, but it is easy to imagine a universe and a people instantly immersed in a religious way of life. There are trees in this universe and they might tell a man in his own secret heart that they like to dwell near his hut. Also chickens and birds and rivers and sunsets and everything that flows and lives. A man in such a world takes his own time and goes about his affairs peacefully, nor does he have to shout and contort his features about the tree which indicated that it liked living near him. His whole world, says Professor Mbiti, is his religion and he is a religious man. This unity and feeling of at-oneness with all living things is the base of African traditional life and one has only to have lived through all kinds of clap-trap and then be plunged into a traditional society to fully support his view. It is indeed as though God, and a very original God, is quietly managing affairs 'behind the scenes,' and people can afford to get on with the task of living. You can't imagine a God here who is only greeted on Sunday or Friday, but Someone who is absorbed and accommodated into a whole social structure and can be greeted at any moment . . . 'Wherever the African is, there is his religion: he carries it to the fields where he is sowing seeds or harvesting a new crop; he takes it with him to the beer party or to attend a funeral ceremony . . .'

I take this view a little further. To me, this is the religion and attitude of mind of any people who have never been wanted by the rest of mankind, nor had the means or education to find God in a posh place. We had to make do with just what was at hand and if God is a subconscious process in our minds, he is perhaps that much more dignified and respected. He is not exclusive either, but shares in every aspect of communal life; that is, the word religion in the traditional sense simply means the way a particular tribe is living from day to day and season to season and year to year . . . 'A great number of beliefs and practices are to be found in any African society. These are not, however, formulated into any systematic set of dogmas which a person is expected to accept. People simply assimilate whatever religious ideas and practices are held or observed by their families and communities . . . and each generation takes them up with modifications suitable to its own historical situation and needs . . .'

One would pause and ponder a little more deeply on his proposition that a communal goodness is the root and foundation of African religion and that the individual within this community derives all his spiritual needs from participating in the entire life of the community. This idea is totally opposed to the great streams of Asian religious ideas where the accent is totally that of individual effort of individual souls. There are superhuman goals set, far above the capabilities of a single man and on examination of those disciplines prescribed, one becomes a little hesitant about the spiritual superman. There are indications of co-operation and assistance from unseen sources, even from that small circle of exclusive disciples, but it is not stressed. The co-operation which is necessary to achieve the highest standards takes a second place to the personalities involved in the propagation of new religious ideas. Thus, the ideas, which are of major importance, fail to become a part of the whole society because not everyone is attracted to a personality.

A great feeling of humility is generated by mutual co-operations: not the individual alone, to the exclusion of everyone else who helped him to become what he is. If this idea was also transported to the realm of the spirit there might be no more caste and class wars in the name of God. Indeed, God in Africa might, at last, be unashamed to say that he is unable to manage the enormous job of being God all by himself. That old man So-and-So with no teeth, but a good heart, gave him a helping hand, so that it is just anybody's heaven, where each person can feel that he matters infinitely and is loved, infinitely. Working his conclusions on the base of the African traditional structure, Professor Mbiti proposes a type of transfused religion. He says: 'Transfused religion is the type which promises the greatest amount of influence on African peoples. Here, religion becomes more and more a social uniformity, without theological depth, personal commitment or martyrs. It is just "there," somewhere in the corpus of one's beliefs, whether one is conscious of being religious or not. It is not *institutionalised* . . . It is equally tolerant as it is indifferent. But this is the form of religious life on which Africa must count to make an impress on morals, ethics, standards, and social conditions of its peoples. *It is a religion behind the scenes.*'

It is this 'behind the scenes' which I like so much, if it could take away the exclusive temples and churches and let God be. After all, God is only there in the first place because people want Something to trust, to feel some organising ability Somewhere, to feel the need for restraint, and perhaps to be loved. Maybe God does these things anyway, whether mankind cares or not, but there was something wrong with the other social structures. One after another they are condemned or doomed as God and caste in India is doomed. The outline Professor Mbiti gives of the African social structures is an invitation to the Gods to try out a new climate: 'In traditional religions there are no creeds to be recited; instead, the creeds are written in the heart of the individual, and each one is himself a living creed of his own religion. Where the individual is, there is his religion, for he is a religious being. It is this that makes Africans so religious: religion is in their whole system of being . . .'

1969

1   John S. Mbiti. *African Religions and Philosophy*. London: Heinemann, 1969.

Despite broken bondage, Botswana women are still unloved

In the old days a woman was regarded as sacred only if she knew her place, which was in her yard with her mother-in-law and children. A number of oppressive traditions, however, completely obliterated her as a thinking, feeling human being and she was exploited in all sorts of ways. So heavy is the toll of the centuries on the women of Botswana, that even with present-day political independence for the country, one finds that the few highly literate women of the country talk in uncertain terms of their lives and fear to assert themselves.

In strongly traditional societies there is a long thread of continuity between the past and the present and one often looks back to the past to explain the social maladies of the present. One of the earliest and surprisingly accurate views of Botswana society was recorded in 1805 by a German traveller,[1] Dr W. H. C. Lichtenstein. Many an old man of the tribe will confirm Dr Lichtenstein's observations. About the position of women in the society, he recorded:

' . . . The husband secures a livelihood by hunting, tending the cattle and milking the cows. When at home he only prepares hides and makes skin coats and cloth for himself and his wife. About the children he hardly cares . . . the gentler sex plays a very inferior part in the life of the tribe . . . It must not be overlooked that this servitude of women is not a consequence of tyranny by men, but due to certain causes, which ameliorate the lot of a Bechuana woman, although it might not be desirable according to our standards. The number of men is relatively small and they have to hunt and go to war, so naturally all the peaceful duties and occupations are done by women. Only such work as can suddenly be dropped and can be interrupted for some length of time, such as sewing of clothes, is done by men. All other work which has to be done continuously such as building, tilling of the soil, the making of pots, baskets, ropes and other household utensils is done by women. Two-thirds of the nation are women and even without any wars they would have to belong to the working class . . .'

It has also been said that a true man in this world did not listen to the opinion of women; under polygamy women shared a husband with one or several other women and the custom of *bogadi* or the offering of a gift of cattle by her husband's family to her own family at the time of marriage, had overtones of complete bondage to a husband and his family and undertones of a sales bargain. But in spite of all this, women have experienced considerable emancipation in Botswana. Their emancipation has never been an applied or intellectual movement; it centres around a number of historical factors, not the least being the complicated and dominant role Christianity played in the political history of the country.

All the tribes in Botswana have a shared history so that it is possible to discuss changes that took place in broad terms. Unlike South Africa, Botswana had a benign form of colonial rule and invasion under the old British Bechuanaland Protectorate established in 1885. Colonial rule was benign for an odd reason – the country was grim and unproductive, subject to recurrent cycles of drought. The British had no interest in it, except as a safe passageway to the interior. British interest was focused on Mashonaland (now Rhodesia), which, they erroneously believed, held huge deposits of gold. Due to this, Botswana remained independent in a way; its customs and traditions were left intact and people's traditional rulers had a large say in governing their people. Thus, the real Southern African dialogues took place in Botswana. Christianity was a dialogue here, as was black people's ownership of the land and the retention of the ancient African land tenure system, as was trade.

It was about 1890 that the iron hand-plough was introduced into the country and this implement played a major role in lightening woman's burden as an all-round food producer. Formerly, women scratched at the earth with a hoe. When the iron plough was introduced it created a small social problem that could only be solved by the men. It was forbidden in custom for women to handle cattle so men were needed to inspan the oxen and pull the plough. Agriculture then became a joint task shared by a man and his family. The peaceful establishment of trade brought a new form of clothing into the country, 'European clothes', which was universally adopted.

Christianity then presented itself as a doctrine above all traditions and mores; a moral choice freely available to both men and women and it is in this sphere that all major social reforms took place. Attention has to be shifted briefly at this point to an area of the country where Christianity and all it implied became the major dialogue. It was in the Bamangwato area of the country, over the years 1866–1875 where a young chief, later known as Khama, The Great, suffered religious persecution from his father, Chief Sekgoma I, for making a complete and absolute conversion to Christian doctrine. This brought Khama into conflict with traditional African custom, which was upheld by his father. The act of suffering persecution for a belief eventually made Khama the victor in the struggle and the leading social reformer of the country. It could also be said of Khama that he was a compassionate man by inclination because some of his reforms, which must have been extremely difficult to initiate, appear to have been motivated entirely by compassion and this is no more evident than in his abolition of *bogadi* or the bride price.

It is significant that of the five major tribes of the country, only the Bomangwato and Batawana completely abolished *bogadi*. All the other tribes still adhere to the custom. People vehemently deny that *bogadi* is the 'purchase of women' and yet central to its functioning is human greed and the acquisition of wealth through cattle. Under *bogadi* marriages are so arranged as to retain cattle wealth within kinship groups, so that young girls were usually married to close relatives, a cousin, a father's brother's son.

Many poignant dramas were played out against this background. Marriage was superficially secure. *Bogadi* made a woman a silent slave and chattel in the home of her in-laws; if she was ill-treated by her mother-in-law or husband, she could not complain. Her parents were always anxious that she do nothing to destroy the marriage in case they lose the *bogadi* cattle offered at the time of marriage. *Bogadi* also bonded over to a woman's husband's family all the children she could bear in her lifetime. As frequently happened, her first husband died and should she acquire children from another man, those children too were claimed by her deceased husband's family. *Bogadi* was eventually abolished in Bamangwato country on these compassionate grounds: that each man ought to be the father of his own children. When Khama abolished *bogadi*, he also, for the first time, allowed women to lodge complaints against their husbands on their own and not through a male sponsor, as was required by custom.

Change and progress has always been of a gentle and subtle nature – the widespread adoption of Christianity gradually eliminated polygamous marriages. At independence in 1966, women were given the right to vote alongside men. They did not have to fight for it. But strangely, this very subtlety makes it difficult to account for the present social crisis. The country is experiencing an almost complete breakdown of family life and a high rate of illegitimate births among the children. No one can account for it. It just happened somewhere along the line. A woman's place is no longer in her yard with her mother-in-law but she finds herself as unloved outside the restrictions of custom, as she was, within it. When I first arrived in Botswana in 1964, women confided to me as follows: 'Botswana men are not nice. When you take up with a man he sleeps with you for two weeks, then he passes you on to his friend, who passes you on to his friend. That is how we live . . .'

Possibly two thirds of the nation are still women and about children procreated under such circumstances, the men hardly care.

1 W. H. C. Lichtenstein. *Foundation Of The Cape & About The Bechuanas*. A. A. Balkema: Cape Town, 1973.

1975

57

Makeba music

'They thought what other people only sing in songs,' said Zhivago of his love for Lara. He could not have meant the run-of-the-mill but the songs Miriam Makeba chose for her repertoire. Who else sings of love and life that has a long thread of continuity and purpose?

I have said so many tentative things about her, out of surprise. I once said that the human voice must have power and authority to be heard and she has this – because of the demands she makes on the concentration. I also came around to the view that she has a great soul and this made her transcend the achievements of anything run-of-the-mill. She could never be cheap entertainment.

That two unlike artists like Pasternak and Makeba eventually said the same, eternal, everlasting things to my heart, appears to me that they travelled a similar road where everything was a mass of pain, confusion, loss and human stupidity. They recorded it all with silent eyes, possessively keeping the beauty in their hearts to themselves, knowing it had no place where false ideals were set up whereby people *had* to live or be shot dead or imprisoned.

We were thinking about other things when wading through the bleak terrain that makes up so much of 'Doctor Zhivago' – there were those detailed, precise recordings of what one peasant said and what another peasant said and the recording goes on and on with ruthless precision. The heart of the writer is not involved and that is half the pain of the book. He was just looking and looking and simply not liking anything he looked at. He was a man slowly having a nervous breakdown because of all the things he had been born with in his heart, that he had been born to have a great love affair, in spite of the revolution; that a love affair conducted amidst total collapse was going to be the only worthwhile achievement of his life. Because nothing prepares you for the shattering beauty of the last pages of the book.

The references to Lara are always small, abrupt sentences tagged onto those eyes which silently watched a hateful and inhuman world. They teeter at the end of a terrifying description of Moscow, overrun with the plague and rats, the secret police, where things like fresh vegetables have gone on the black market and are only obtained at the risk of being deported to Siberia. It is those agonies which dominate. There can't be people there anymore, only terror and insanity. In all this Lara says: 'Yura, I want to tell you something.' He knew, says the author with quiet amusement, she thought she was pregnant.

It holds you for some time, the man's heart which he keeps such a secret, as though he is conducting a silent conspiracy of his own against all those things which are not truth but evil. It's as though his heart and what was in it would eventually acquire the power to make the universe whole and sane again. It has that effect, because once the man breaks down and shows you his secret heart, you can't remember or care any longer what one peasant said or the other peasant said – only those eternal lines: 'Oh, what a love it was, how free, how new, like nothing else on earth!'

The voice of Makeba breaks in on the ear in the same way: Oh, how free, how new, like nothing else on earth!

I think it's the shock of the contrast. This same precise, ruthless recording is going on in Southern Africa of life on a bleak, terrible terrain. One black man said this about losing his family and home overnight and another black man said this and you know that the white man who said that can only increase the terror and insanity because his way of life which coddles him and sets him apart from the rest of mankind, needs it. You know Makeba lived through all of this and recorded it with still, silent eyes but when you turn to her music, some other world reaches you where in all, all this a mother sang a song to her baby about a canary.

It is more than just a song when Makeba sings it. It is her whole life and secret heart which she kept to herself throughout all those years she was a recorder of everything that amounted to rubbish – because that's what evil is: *Rubbish*. It is almost with relief that one listens to her music because it says the true things about Southern Africa, that the children who made up the game song about the pretty new dress are going to survive, that there are people here too, black people, born to have great love affairs, full of wonders and things, which will be more important than our revolutions.

I have no logical argument as to why those things are more important, except that I believe in the contents of the human heart, especially when that heart was a silent and secret conspiracy against all the insanity and hatred in mankind. In this context, the heart of Pasternak is the true liberator of Russia and Makeba music is the liberator of all black people.

They could have said other things because we were thinking of other things. But they are greater than others because the end products of both their gifts to mankind is only what they were born with in their hearts.

1977

NOTES ON NOVELS

□

I believe that people cannot protest against evil social systems. The people who create it merely laugh in your face, and keep guns at hand to annihilate you. I believe that the white man in South Africa does not deserve the privilege he is at present enjoying of ruling and being the dominant race of the country because he has not the faintest inkling of how to treat other people, who differ from him in looks, decently.

If you protest and make one gain against apartheid, the South African government, possibly, in terror, has to pass two more repressive laws to liquidate your gain and you end up by increasing the suffering of the people in the country . . . It involves a broader question than mere protest – it is a question of evil as a whole. We are likely to remove one horror and replace it with another and those of us who have suffered much do not relish the endless wail of human misery.

My writing is not on anybody's bandwagon. It is on the sidelines where I can more or less think things out with a clear head. We may be at a turning point and need new names for human dignity, new codes of honour all nations can abide by.

Reply to Index on Censorship **1975**

Some notes on novel writing

Twenty-seven years of my life was lived in South Africa but I have been unable to record this experience in any direct way, as a

61

writer. A very disturbing problem is that we find ourselves born into a situation where people are separated into sharp racial groups. All the people tend to think only in those groups in which they are and one is irked by the artificial barriers. It is as though, with all those divisions and signs, you end up with no people at all. The environment completely defeated me, as a writer. I just want people to be people, so I had no way of welding all the people together into a cohesive whole.

I have attempted to solve my problem by at least writing in an environment where all the people are welded together by an ancient order. Life in Botswana cannot be compared in any way to life in South Africa because here people live very secure lives, in a kind of social order shaped from centuries past by the ancestors of the tribe. I have tended to derive a feeling of security from this, so I could not be considered as a South African writer in exile, but as one who has put down roots. And yet, certain strength in me, certain themes I am likely to write about, have been mainly shaped by my South African experience.

Most of my novels published so far could be said to be didactic works; they were arranged from pre-planned conclusions and principles. I knew what I was preaching against and simply went ahead and preached. What has created difficulties is the source from which I have preached; my message always seemed larger than Botswana so that I seem to have ended up with a Botswana of my own making. I think my situation can best be described in the words of a Jewish artist, Josef Herman, with whom I was slightly acquainted a few years ago. Josef Herman had lived through the Nazi invasion of Poland, then fled as a refugee to England. He chose to settle in a small Welsh mining village and for many years painted portraits of the villagers which were all of the same kind. He painted his landscapes very small but the people in those landscapes were enormously large. They were always quietly and absent-mindedly staring into space. He described his work of this period in words that made a great impact on me. He said: 'A voice seemed to cry out in me for a new name for human dignity.' I found a similar peace in Botswana village life and also drew large and disproportionate portraits of ordinary people. I meant that the immense suffering black people experience in South Africa had created in me a reverence for ordinary people.

I think that our only education in South Africa, as black people, is a political one. We learn bitterly, every day, the details of oppression and exploitation so that a writer automatically feels pressured into taking a political stand of some kind or identifying with a camp. It was important to my development to choose a broader platform for my work, so I have avoided political camps and ideologies because I feel that they falsify truth. It was necessary for me to concentrate directly on people because I believe it is only people who make people suffer and not some hidden, unknown God or devil.

If all my living experience could be summarised I would call it knowledge of evil, knowledge of its sources, of its true face and the misery and suffering it inflicts on human life. I have always tended to work with great force and authority; all my conclusions are sweeping ones based on learning and experience. Certain insights I had gained into the nature of evil were initially social ones, based entirely on my South African experience. I welcomed any social order or individual who represented broad and unselfish planning for everyone. I later worked deeper than that, bringing the problem of evil closer to my own life. I found myself in a situation where there was no guarantee against the possibility that I could be evil too. I found that one earns only a slight guarantee against the possibility of inflicting harm on others through an experience which completely destroys one's own ego or sense of self-esteem. This can be so devastating that one is not likely to survive it. I had tended to leave my work at that stage with rough outlines of good and evil, which either I or someone else might fill in at a later stage. What has driven me is a feeling that human destiny ought not to proceed along tragic lines, with every effort and every new-born civilisation throttling itself in destruction with wrong ideas and wrong ways of living.

These trends of thought have very much occupied my writing life. I spent a whole portion of my life in a country where it was

63

impossible for black people to dream, so I know what that's like. I spent another portion in a country where it is possible to dream and I have combined these two different experiences in my writing.

I know that my first novel, *When Rain Clouds Gather*, was my most amateur effort. Harmless and amateur as it is, the book has a certain value for me. When I first arrived in Botswana in 1964, I was entirely dependent on what the people of the country communicated to me. The major talking point at that time was a terrible drought in which 300,000 cattle died. The other issue was the first general election for independence. I think only a South African-born black person could fully appreciate the situation. It meant that here, if black people were faced with a national calamity that affected them deeply, they could form little cattle co-operatives to resolve their distress; a co-operative of any kind in South Africa would cause a riot of hysteria among the white population – their wealth and privilege are dependent on the poverty and distress of black people. It meant that here, all the people could vote for a government of their own choice, which would presumably care for their interests and welfare. Black people will never vote for a government of their own choice in South Africa. So Makhaya's entry into Botswana, as a refugee, was like sending a message back to his own home; this is what we really ought to have.

I have found that the novel form is like a large rag-bag into which one can stuff anything – all one's philosophical, social and romantic speculations. I have always reserved a special category for myself, as a writer – that of a pioneer blazing a new trail into the future. It would seem as though Africa rises at a point in history when world trends are more hopefully against exploitation, slavery and oppression – all of which has been synonymous with the name, Africa. I have recorded whatever hopeful trend was presented to me in an attempt to shape the future, which I hope will be one of dignity and compassion.

1978

Social and political pressures that shape writing in Southern Africa

In some inexplicable way the South American writer, Gabriel Garcia Marquez, captured the whole soul of ancient Southern African history in a few casual throw-away lines in his novel *One Hundred Years of Solitude*:

> . . . In the small separate room, where the walls were gradually being covered by strange maps and fabulous drawings, he taught them to read and write and do sums, and he spoke to them about the wonders of the world, not only where his learning had extended, but forcing the limits of his imagination to extremes. It was in that way that the boys ended up learning that in the southern extremes of Africa there were men so intelligent and peaceful that their only pastime was to sit and think . . .[1]

This astonishing observation on life in Southern Africa occurs at the very beginning of the novel and except that insofar as it is indicative of the author's vast range of intellectual compassion, the quote I use is quite unrelated to the general development of the novel's themes and preoccupations. What is so astonishing is the accuracy of the observation. Southern African history is associated with so many horrors – police states, detentions, sudden and violent mass protests and death, exploitation and degrading political systems. Any thought that it could have once been one of 'the wonders of the world' seems unreal.

And yet, long ago, before the period of colonial invasion, it was a beautiful world. The British historian, Anthony Sillery, in his book *Founding a Protectorate*, gives a little indication of life in Southern Africa before it was almost totally conquered by foreign powers:

> . . . at the beginning of the Scramble for Africa the southern route presented to Great Britain the most readily available means of access to the interior . . . Southern Africa, especially for an Englishman, was a friendly country. The chiefs, many of

them courteous, civilised men, were hospitable, and the people helpful and only rarely aggressive . . .[2]

Sillery contrasts this with the difficulties the invaders faced in their attempts to conquer East and North Western Africa. The tribes were generally 'rapacious, suspicious, extortionate and warlike and the interior filled with steamy, fetid swamps through which nothing but a canoe could travel.'

I was born in South Africa and that is synonymous with saying that one is born into a very brutal world − if one is black. Everything had been worked out by my time and the social and political life of the country was becoming harsher and harsher. A sense of history was totally absent in me and it was as if, far back in history, thieves had stolen the land and were so anxious to cover up all traces of the theft that correspondingly, all traces of the true history have been obliterated. We, as black people, could make no appraisal of our own worth; we did not know who or what we were, apart from objects of abuse and exploitation. Each nation offers the world a little of its light; each nation boasts of the great men who shaped its destiny. We had a land that offered the world only gold; no great men were needed to articulate the longings of the people. In a creative sense I found myself left only with questions. How do we and our future generations resolve our destiny? How do we write about a world long since lost, a world that never seemed meant for humans in the first place, a world that reflected only misery and hate? It was my attempt to answer some of these questions that created many strange divergences in my own work.

Botswana is so close to South Africa that barely a night's journey by train separates the two countries from each other. Botswana was the former British Bechuanaland Protectorate which became independent in 1966. In my eyes Botswana is the most unique and distinguished country in the whole of Africa. It has a past history that is unequalled anywhere in Africa. It is a land that was never conquered or dominated by foreign powers and so a bit of ancient Africa, in all its quiet and unassertive grandeur, has remained intact there. It became my home in 1964.

When I was first published in 1968, a London literary agent wrote to me as follows: '. . . There isn't much of a market for South African literature here in England. People don't seem to be so interested in it. But you have new experiences by having lived in Botswana. Let us see what you can make of it . . .'

I cannot pretend to be a student of South African literature; I cannot assess its evolution or lack of evolution. I only feel sure that the main function of a writer is to make life magical and to communicate a sense of wonder. I do admit that I found the South African situation so evil that it was impossible for me to deal with, in creative terms. A British visitor to South Africa once said to me: 'You arrive in South Africa and see all those black faces. And you think: "They must have the same sensitivities and feelings as we do." But no matter how much you think this the system beams at you that all those black faces are not human and you leave the country without having any communication with black people at all . . .'

It was this nightmare sense of despair that was suddenly lifted from me. Literature is very functional in Southern Africa and bound inextricably to human suffering; the death of South African literature is that it is almost blinded by pain; people hardly exist beside the pain. I found myself performing a peculiar shuttling movement between two lands. All my work had Botswana settings but the range and reach of my preoccupations became very wide. People, black people, white people, loomed large on my horizon. I began to answer some of the questions aroused by my South African experience.

My work has covered the whole spectrum of Southern African preoccupations – refugeeism, racialism, patterns of evil, and the ancient Southern African historical dialogue.

Refugeeism. Refugees flood into Botswana from three points – South West Africa (Namibia), Rhodesia (Zimbabwe), and South Africa. In 1967 I was officially registered as a South African refugee and for two years I lived with the refugee community in Northern Botswana. My first novel, *When Rain Clouds Gather*, grew out of this experience. It was a fearfully demoralising way of life, of unemployment and hand-outs from the World Council of

Churches. Liberation and power loomed large on the horizon for refugees from Zimbabwe and due to this they were the only refugees at that time who were regularly air-lifted out of Botswana for military training. They were all in opposing camps and their quarrels about power were violent and brutal. A young refugee from Zimbabwe quietly detached himself from the group and held long dialogues with me. He wanted an alternative to war and power. He had no faith in the future black leadership of Zimbabwe. There was no one articulating the hopes of the people and he did not want to die for a worthless cause. I latched eagerly on to his dialogue and my first novel provides an alternative for young men. I created a symbolic type of refugee personality. I implied that he was a man of talent. I made him briefly face the implications of black power and then turned him abruptly away from the madding crowd to spend a lifetime in a small rural village, battling with food production problems.

My first novel is important to me in a personal way. It is my only truly South African work, reflecting a black South African viewpoint. The central character in the novel, a black South African refugee, is almost insipid, a guileless, simple-hearted simpleton. But that is a true reflection of the black South African personality. We are an oppressed people who have been stripped bare of every human right. We do not know what it is like to have our ambitions aroused, nor do we really see liberation on an immediate horizon. Botswana was a traumatic experience to me and I found the people, initially, extremely brutal and harsh, only in the sense that I had never encountered human ambition and greed before in a black form.

Racialism. With all my South African experience I longed to write an enduring novel on the hideousness of racial prejudice. But I also wanted the book to be so beautiful and so magical that I, as the writer, would long to read and re-read it. I achieved this ambition in an astonishing way in my second novel, *Maru.* In Botswana they have a conquered tribe, the Basarwa or Bushmen. It is argued that they were the true owners of the land in some distant past, that they had been conquered by the more powerful Botswana tribes and from then onwards assumed the traditional role of slaves. Basarwa people were also abhorrent to Botswana people because they hardly looked African, but Chinese. I knew the language of racial hatred but it was an evil exclusively practised by white people. I therefore listened in amazement as Botswana people talked of the Basarwa whom they oppressed:

'They don't think,' they said. 'They don't know anything.'

For the first time I questioned blind prejudice:

'How do they know that? How can they be sure that the Basarwa are not thinking?'

The research I did among Botswana people for *Maru* gave me the greatest insights and advantages to work right at the roots of racial hatred. I found out above all that that type of exploitation and evil is dependent on a lack of communication between the oppressor and the people he oppresses. It would horrify an oppressor to know that his victim has the same longings, feelings, and sensitivities as he has. Nothing prevented a communication between me and Botswana people and nothing prevented me from slipping into the skin of a Mosarwa person. And so my novel was built up in blinding flashes of insights into an evil that hung like the sickness of death over all black people in South Africa.

Patterns of Evil. My third novel, *A Question of Power*, had such an intensely personal and private dialogue that I can hardly place it in the context of the more social and outward-looking work I had done. It was a private philosophical journey to the sources of evil. I argued that people and nations do not realise the point at which they become evil; but once trapped in its net, evil has a powerful propelling motion into a terrible abyss of destruction. I argued that its form, design, and plan could be clearly outlined and that it was little understood as a force in the affairs of mankind.

The Ancient Southern African Historical Dialogue. If one wishes to reach back into ancient Africa, the quality of its life has been preserved almost intact in Botswana. It is a world that moves so slowly that it seems to be asleep within itself. It is like a broad, deep, unruffled river and as accommodating. Anything that falls into its depth is absorbed. No new idea stands sharply aloof from the social body, declaiming its superiority. It is absorbed and transformed until it emerges somewhere along the line as 'our traditional custom.' Everything is touched by 'our traditional custom' – British Imperialism, English, Independence, new educational methods, progress, and foreigners. It all belongs. So deep is people's sense of security that their general expression is one of abstraction and quiet absent-mindedness.

Botswana is one of those countries that survive by sheer luck and unexpected good fortune. On several occasions it teetered on the brink of being absorbed into Rhodesia or being governed by South Africa. During the period of colonial occupation, it produced two of the greatest black leaders the continent may ever know – Khama, The Great, and his son, Tshekedi Khama – men distinguished for their personal integrity and the power with which they articulated the hopes of their people. During the period of colonial occupation the British scoured the land from end to end in an endeavour to uncover its mineral wealth. Accidentally, after independence, the largest diamond mine in the world was discovered by a jet plane photographing the Kalahari desert with an infra-red light camera. It is thought that had the British still been in control they would have wrecked the country rather than forsake such wealth.

Botswana benefited by the catastrophe which fell upon South Africa. At the time of exploration into the interior all black chiefs were illiterate. They were helplessly dependent on verbal explanations given to them about documents which appealed for gold and diamond exploration concession rights. The verbal explanations never tallied with the contents of the documents, which dealt with the wholesale purchase of the land by the foreign invaders. In African custom the land could never be bought or sold; it could be apportioned for use to foreigners who had been befriended by the tribe or who had rendered services. The above and many other fraudulent means, like intoxicating the chiefs with brandy and then getting them to sign concession documents, were used to wrest the land from the tribes. Most of the tribes of South Africa were landless by the 1830s when foreign invasion reached the southern tip of Botswana.

Then a reaction set in. The powerful London Missionary Society which had its headquarters at Kuruman, near the southern tip of Botswana, began to campaign about the land question. Missionaries like John Mackenzie wrote books and papers exposing the means by which the land had been taken from black people and the suffering which ensued. The land question and almost every other question relevant to the black man's destiny converged in Botswana. It is on record that the British did not want Botswana. In their despatches they called it 'a God-awful country to live in.' It was grim and unproductive, subject to seven-year cycles of severe drought. It was called the 'thirstland' by the early explorers as surface water was almost non-existent. Eventually, the country was given a general blanket coverage of 'British Protection' because its only advantage to the British was that the land was almost uniformly level and provided an ideal situation for a railway line through to the interior. Apart from the railway line, they left the land and the people intact and undisturbed. Botswana uniquely remained black man's country.

The people could still have been destroyed by so many hostile forces – the northward thrust of the Afrikaner Boer, the Germans and the Portuguese. It was not the British who sought out Botswana but the people of Botswana who sought out the British. A vague feeling floated in the air at that time that it was only the British who could be trusted to have honest dealings with black people. Yes, where financial greed was not a major British concern, the British took time off to hold exquisite dialogues of integrity.

Corresponding to the time of the declaration of the British Protectorate, Botswana produced a leader of such magnificence, Khama III or Khama, the Great, that the British bowed in awe and deference before him. His standards of integrity were so high that the British conceded to him what they would not concede to any black man at that time – a voice in Britain during the scramble for Africa. Thus, the details of foreign occupation were meticulously worked out. Although the country attracted few white settlers due to the harshness of its climate, the few who came in entered on tiptoe and minded their p's and q's. Khama III

71

established a tradition whereby the chiefs of the land maintained a control over government and trade and he also retained the right, during his rule, to deport any white settler or missionary who displeased him.

The people of the land were never exposed to or broken by the sheer stark horror of white domination. They kept on dreaming as from ancient times and they kept alive the portrait of ancient Africa. It was this peaceful world of black people simply dreaming in their own skins that I began to slowly absorb into my own life. It was like finding black power and black personality in a simple and natural way. If the country is destroyed in the post-independence years, it will be by horrors within itself and not by foreign powers.

1   Gabriel Garcia Marquez. *One Hundred Years of Solitude.* Harmondsworth: Penguin, 1972, p.20.
2   Anthony Sillery. *Founding a Protectorate: History of Bechuanaland.* The Hague: Mouton, 1965, p.70.

1979

A note on Rain Clouds[1]

Over the years 1967 to 1968 I was a part of the refugee community in northern Botswana.

At that time liberation and power loomed large on the horizon only for refugees from Rhodesia and large amounts of young men were regularly airlifted out of Botswana by their political organisations for military training. So the pressure was all going one way towards the liberatory war. The young men awaiting air-lifts were all in opposing camps and their quarrels about power were violent and brutal.

Under the circumstances then it can be said that I record the dialogues of the wrong sorts of people, who, as the liberatory war pattern unfolded in Zimbabwe, tended to resist certain pressures in the military camps or express an idealism which cost them their life. *When Rain Clouds Gather* was built up out of this kind of material. A young refugee from Zimbabwe quietly detached himself from the group and held long dialogues with me. He didn't want to go for military training. He had no faith in the future black leadership of Zimbabwe because there was no one articulating the hopes of the people and he did not want to die for a worthless cause.

This is the sort of thing no one plans for in Africa: the possibility that Africa can produce a lot of idealist young men, the need for broad planning for the people to solve centuries of exploitation and poverty. There is only a wild rush for power and a kind of war of extermination of anyone who is a threat to those who seek power. I tended to be caught in the intensity of this dialogue and for a long time (through three novels) held on to the same theme. I would deliberately create heroes and show their extreme willingness to abdicate from positions of power and absorb themselves in activities which would be of immense benefit to people.

In each instance the horizon of African liberation has been narrowed down to horrific power struggles that destroy one country after another. I built an horizon in which black men of talent were portrayed in activities which were 'a new beginning'. I wanted to widen the images on that horizon and to give young black men alternative choices. It was like a suggestion I hoped would move into the future while not too much could be done about the chaos of the present.

1 Parts of this piece overlap with passages from the foregoing essay. However, there are some additional comments of significance in this piece that warrant its inclusion here.

1979

3

Retrospect:

Southern Africa
and Beyond
1979–1986

Notes from a quiet backwater II

I need a quiet backwater and a sense of living as though I am barely alive on the earth, treading a small, careful pathway through life.

All my work is scaled down to this personality need, with the universe itself seen through the eyes of small, individual life dramas.

My earlier work was filled with personal data and responses to challenges that were on the whole internal and private. I feel that people, insofar as they are able, need to have a sense of alertness about destiny, a sort of alertness about their spiritual history.

The canvas on which I have worked was influenced by a belief in the Hindu view of rebirth and reincarnation. Such a belief influences one to the view that each individual, no matter what their present origin or background may be, is really the total embodiment of human history, with a vast accumulation of knowledge and experience stored in the subconscious mind.

It was against this background of an individual who could possibly have lived a million other lives, in a million different circumstances, that I began to view my relationship to Africa.

The African experience of slavery, colonialism and exploitation arouses feelings of intense anguish and there was a fear in me that monsters would merely change roles, that black faces would simply replace white faces of cruelty, hate and greed and that the people would bleed forever.

It was as though, in an internal and private way, I perceived the ease with which one could become evil and I associated evil in my mind with the acquisition of power.

This terror of power and an examination of its stark horrors created a long period of anguish in my life and forced out of me some strange novels that I had not anticipated writing.

It was almost as though the books wrote themselves, propelled into existence by the need to create a reverence for human life in an environment and historical circumstances that seem to me a howling inferno.

Thus, all my earlier work was concerned with stating personal choices and there was an anxiety in them that those personal choices be the right ones.

Manipulated characters talk anxiously for the author. The dialogue begins tentatively and simply in my first novel.

The male character, who obligingly serves the author, has two possible destinies; one being of fame and importance.

He is forced to choose beautifully: 'I shall choose the road of peace of mind. I shall choose a quiet backwater and work together with people.'

This initial simple dialogue and choice became more and more complex in my other two novels. It was as though beautiful, simple choices stirred up all the wrath of demons in hell.

They seemed to be shouting at me: 'No, no, no. We don't want that. We are here to enrich ourselves at the expense of the people. We want you to be like us, else you will spoil everything.'

The earlier work was written over a period of such high inner distress with repetitive cycles of nervous breakdowns that on looking back I feel that the learning recorded in them defined my relationship to Africa, not only in one life but in other lives to come.

Having defined the personal, my work became more social and outward-looking.

The history of Southern Africa fascinates me, not necessarily the miserable history of the Great Trek, the land-grabbing, cattle-grabbing wars and the diamond and gold rushes, but themes that are linked to the eternal stream of mankind's history.

Much of mankind's history would seem so similar, rather than dissimilar – the sparsely furnished hut, the agricultural and pastoral rhythm and the religions based on ritual murder.

I have been fortunate in that I have lived for a long period in the rural parts of Botswana where life is a little bit of everything and where people were ruled for 80 years by an indifferent and almost absent colonial power.

The British tended to leave the society and culture almost intact and traces of many ancient traditions and courtesies still remain in the society.

It is in such pockets of peace that one slowly builds up a continuous portrait of African history.

I think that many writers, in reaction against the humiliation of the colonial era, would like to build up an image of Africa, other than the humble humility of the sparsely furnished hut.

Some of one's work is like reclaiming that humility that has been trampled on and abused.

The words of a French philosopher, Simone Weil, run rather true to the European invasion of Africa:

> 'In the course of the ages a great many invasions have succeeded each other. Each time that the invader has given himself up to the spirit of the place and has drunk of its inspiration, there has been a civilisation. Each time that he preferred to maintain his proud ignorance, there has been barbarism, and darkness worse than death has covered the land for centuries . . .'

1982

Foreword to Sol Plaatje's
Native Life in South Africa

It is possible that no other legislation has so deeply affected the lives of black people in South Africa as the Natives' Land Act of 1913. It created overnight a floating landless proletariat whose labour could be used and manipulated at will, and ensured that ownership of the land had finally and securely passed into the hands of the ruling white race. On it rest the pass laws, the migratory labour system, influx control and a thousand other evils which affect the lives of black people in South Africa today. The passing of the Natives' Land Act was devastating enough to evoke, for the first time, organised black protest of an intellectual kind. It stirred into existence the newly-founded South African Native National Congress (which later became the African National

79

Congress) and gave voice to a new class, a black elite educated for the most part by missionaries in the British liberal tradition.

Sol Plaatje writes of an era in South African history almost unknown to succeeding generations. The wars for the land – spear and shield against cannon and gun – are over and he unfolds the history of a mute and subdued black nation who had learned to call the white man 'baas'. The population at that time is about one and a quarter million whites to about five million blacks. The black population is domiciled and occupied in various ways – in locations and reserves, in urban areas, in public service building roads and railways, or working on farms. But in vast tracts of the rural areas of the Cape Colony, the Orange Free State and the Transvaal, a kind of zamindari system is in operation. About one million black people are squatters on 'European' farms. Having no land of their own, they hire a farm, or grazing and ploughing rights, from the white landowner. It is this population of one million squatters on European farms who are immediately hard hit by the Natives' Land Act.

Prior to the introduction of the Natives' Land Act of 20 June 1913, the Pass Law was introduced for the first time on 28 February 1913. Its aims were to prohibit black people from wandering about without a proper pass, from squatting on farms, from sowing on the share crop system. It facilitated the introduction of the Natives' Land Act. There were two reasons for the introduction of the Natives' Land Act: black farming was proving to be too competitively successful as against white farming and there was a demand for a flow of cheap labour to the gold mines. As long as black men were engaged in farming and were independent owners of livestock, their labour was hard to acquire. An attempt had been made in 1904 to solve the labour crisis in the gold mines by the importing of Chinese labour to do unskilled work in the mines; an initial 43,000 such labourers were imported. At first gold output leapt upwards but conditions on the mines and in the compounds – low wages and flogging with many men driven to practise sodomy in their desperate need for sexual release – led to strikes, robbery and murder. All Chinese labour was deported back to China in 1910.

Thus, some parts of the Natives' Land Act were shaped by the desperate need for labour on the mines. The Act summarily demanded the eviction of one million black tenants on the farms, together with their livestock and all they might own. It was unlawful to have black tenants, but lawful to have black servants. Once a servant, the black man's cattle worked henceforth for the white landlord, free of charge. Any white landowner who failed to comply with the law faced a fine of £100 or six months' imprisonment. Rather than lose their last shred of independence, thousands of black people, tenants on the land, took to the road with their dying stock. On no part of South African soil could they graze or water their animals. Sol Plaatje was at that time editor of a newspaper, *Tsala ea Batho (The People's Friend)* at Kimberley and he took to the road too, compiling first hand information on the plight of these wandering refugees. These sections, which he calls 'that black July' and a deliberate act of genocide, form the most moving chapters of the book.

But *Native Life* is wide and deep in its historical reach. A full portrait of the times emerges and we are presented with a view of history reaching back nearly five hundred years and up to a period of change and transition as it has affected the lives of black people. Plaatje acknowledges that black people have no power so his main aim is to present the black personality as deserving justice, humanity and dignity. He appeals to a higher power, in this instance Britain, and is passionately pro-British in all his arguments:

> The Britishers' vocabulary includes that sacred word Home – and that, perhaps, is the reason why their colonising schemes have always allowed some tracts of country for native family life, with reasonable opportunities for their future existence and progress, in the vast South African expanses . . . In 1910, much against our will, the British Government surrendered its immediate sovereignty over our land to colonials and cosmopolitan aliens who know little about Home, because their dictionaries contain no such loving term . . .

He contrasts this eloquent plea to a more humane power with an outline of another power of stunted spiritual and intellectual growth which he fears will dominate the land – the Afrikaner Boer.

> . . . The northward march of the Voortrekkers was a gigantic plundering raid. They swept like a desolating pestilence through the land, blasting everything in their path and pitilessly laughing at ravages from which the native races have not yet recovered . . .

The state of Union and indeed the passing of the Natives' Land Act represented the triumph of this gross, brute spirit. How deep this triumph has been, history itself has borne out, for South Africa is a land where history proceeds up to the present day in events of unrelieved horror, untouched by human tenderness, charm and unpredictability.

An insistent theme of the book is that black people have no representation in Parliament. They do not have the right to vote – that right is limited to white men only; therefore black people cannot accept the legislation of a parliament that bears no responsibility towards black men.

The South African Native National Congress appointed a deputation of five men, of whom Plaatje was one of those nominated, to appeal to Britain for a repeal of the Natives' Land Act. Predictably, the appeal failed. South Africa was self-governing and independent and Britain a remote power, cool and indifferent, where satisfaction at the outcome of fateful planning that had been conducted for months on end was hinted at in undertones.

Native Life does not fail as a book of flaming power and energy, astonishingly crowded with data of the day-to-day life of a busy man who assumed great sorrows and great responsibilities, who felt himself fully representative of a silent, oppressed people and by sheer grandeur of personality, honoured that obligation. Most black South Africans suffer from a very broken sense of history. *Native Life* provides an essential, missing link. This book may have failed to appeal to human justice in its time, but there is in its tears, anguish and humility, an appeal to a day of retribution.

1982

The old iron cooking pot of Europe

◆

In every homestead in rural Botswana and indeed in many homes in Southern Africa, there is a remarkable cooking pot – the tripod, made entirely of iron with a round belly and resting on the ground on three stands or legs. The pot is of all sizes. For everyday household meals a small wood fire is lit directly under a medium size pot and it is as though the pot itself is a small portable cooking stove producing endless meals of boiled meat and porridge. For wedding feasts and funerals where large numbers of people have to be fed, immense versions of the iron pot are brought out and great log fires are lit under the pot to cook the enormous meals.

A cooking pot may seem a mundane and impossible subject to discuss but I am fascinated by history, by the migrations of people, by the meeting of many strange cultures and by trade and the exchange of goods. I had always associated the tripod, the open outdoor fireplace and its simple humility, with the lives of black people. It never occurred to me that the cooking pot was an imported item and had at some stage in history travelled thousands of miles over oceans to become an indispensable part of African homesteads.

Trade can change a whole way of life. At one stage it was necessary for me to attempt to reconstruct the self-sufficient traditional African society where people had produced all their own household goods. It was a difficult task as few of the traditional items have survived. The clay pots were fragile and so were the knives, axes and spears. They were rapidly discarded in favour of European goods. I interviewed an old woman who was one of the last clay pot makers in the village. The skill of being a clay pot maker had been transmitted to her by her mother but she had no daughter or grand-daughter who was interested in learning the skill.

A hundred years ago, being a housewife in traditional African society was a highly skilled occupation. Women had to know how to produce many household items like clay pots and baskets for storing grain; they also had to plough the fields and produce the year's supply of corn, thatch and build the walls of mud huts. Today women simply buy sturdy galvanised iron buckets and other household items from the shops. But the old clay pot maker told me: 'In the old days my clay pots were not only used to draw water. They were cooking pots as well.' I remember being astonished that such a fragile item as a clay pot, worked at patiently by hand and fired roughly over a home-made kiln, could be used for cooking. The interview also created a nagging worry in my mind. If clay pots had been cooking pots in the old days, where did the tripod come from? The tripods seemed such a traditional African household item that I failed to press the old people about their origins.

The answer to my worry came in a surprising way. I took a trip to Denmark and one evening I was taken out to a restaurant in Copenhagen for a meal. The restaurant was done up in the decor of an old-style Danish farmhouse. My hostess said to me: 'Our ancestors used an open hearth for cooking and an iron pot hung down by a chain from the chimney.'

The iron pot was missing from the decor but she quickly drew a sketch of it. It was the tripod that had travelled so far from its original home, Europe, and found another home on the African continent. Its usefulness as a cooking pot may be over in Europe but it is still very much alive on thousands of African hearths.

A long line of speculation followed. I thought that it would only be the Dutch Trek Boer, whose original home was Holland, who had first introduced the tripod and many other items of trade to black people. In 1837 there was a massive migration of Trek Boers from British rule at the Cape on account of Britain's abolition of the slave trade and general dissatisfaction with British rule. The British were uninterested in the interior of Africa at that time as they were involved in the conquest of India. Thus it was that the Trek Boers were the first of the European races to have contact with black people in the interior of Southern Africa and to introduce new items of trade. The items of trade introduced to black people were so new that there were no equivalents for them in African languages. Dutch or Afrikaans names for a trading item

84

were absorbed directly into many African languages in Southern Africa. For example:

Setswana	Afrikaans	English
suikere	suiker	sugar
nekere	lekkers	sweets
broek	broek	trousers
goude	goud	gold
tee	tee	tea

I can speculate endlessly on the sense of wonder that must have filled black people on being presented with a wide range of goods like cooking pots, ploughs, knives and axes, sturdier and more durable than the goods produced by their ancestors. But a meeting of strange cultures in Southern Africa did not inspire wonder and communication between black and white. It produced a desolate history of moans, lamentations and wars. For a long while the concerns of black people and their day to day survival were of little account. It may have been an historic moment when the first tripod from Europe appeared in black homesteads, sturdier than the clay pot the ancestors had produced before. I thought I would record a little of its history because it fills me with wonder.

1983

A search for historical continuity and roots

In March 1964, barely a day's journey separated me from one way of life and another. Until that day in March I had been a South African citizen. A very peripheral involvement in politics resulted in a refusal of a passport and I left South Africa on an exit permit. Great events were taking place then. Most of Africa was gaining independence and I was a part of the stirring of the times. It was consciously in my mind that African independence had to be defined in the broadest possible terms. I was twenty-seven years old and had lived those years like most black South Africans, an

85

urban slum dweller who survived precariously, without a sense of roots, without a sense of history. A short train journey and a day later I awoke to a completely new world, Botswana, (then the British Bechuanaland Protectorate) and a way of life unknown and unfamiliar to me. South Africa, with its sense of ravages and horror, has lost that image of an Africa, ancient and existing since time immemorial, but in Botswana the presence of the timeless and immemorial is everywhere – in people, in animals, in everyday life and in custom and tradition.

I hope two disparate worlds could be considered to have combined harmoniously in me. I have never been able in my writing to represent South African society but the situation of black people in South Africa, their anguish and their struggles, made its deep impress on me. From an earlier background, I know of a deep commitment to people, an involvement in questions of poverty and exploitation and a commitment to illuminating the future for younger generations. I needed an eternal and continuous world against which to work out these preoccupations. One of my preoccupations was a search as an African for a sense of historical continuity, a sense of roots, but I remember how tentative and sketchy were my first efforts, not finding roots as such but rather putting on layer after layer of patchy clothing. This patchy clothing formed the background to most of my work.

It was my habit to walk slowly through the village and observe the flow of everyday life – newly-cut thatch glowing like a golden hay-stack on a round mud hut, children racing around, absorbed in their eternal games or a woman busy pounding corn for the evening meal. I would pause a while near a yard where a tall, slender woman pounded corn in a stamping block with a long wooden pestle, her bare feet partly buried in a growth of summer grass. It was a scene that had been a part of village life since time immemorial but to me it was as fresh and new as creation itself. The woman's form would sway to and fro with the rhythm of her work, her face closed and withdrawn in concentration. The warm slanting rays of the late afternoon sunlight seemed to transfix that timeless moment in my memory. I would turn and look at the distant horizon. Beyond the last hut, beyond the perimeter of

Serowe, the land lay in an eternal, peaceful sleep, the distant horizon hazy and shrouded in the mists of the earth. I would reflect that the dwelling places of all the tribes had been, for ages and ages, just such small, self-contained worlds, busy with the everyday round of living.

Such peaceful rural scenes would be hastily snatched to form the backdrop to tortuous novels. Perceptive fans sensed the disparity, the disparity between the peaceful simplicity of village life and a personality more complex than village life could ever be. They would say: 'I like the bits about Botswana life but I found your second/third novel difficult to read . . .'

But it still goes back to a question of roots rather than the small, stolen patchy scenes which would seem implicit in my early work. Later, much later, I became acquainted with the history of Botswana and it was like becoming acquainted with a way of life that was applicable to all the tribes of Africa. The high clamour and violence of South African history dominates all the southern lands so that they are written of in the history books as mere appendages of South African history. Botswana is no mere extension of South African history and the great arid wasteland the history books would have us believe. It was a British Protectorate and as such has a distinct and individual history of its own, a history whereby a colonial power was sensitive to human grandeur, even if it turned up in a black skin, and it was a country that provided one such leader at a crucial moment, Khama the Great, who made known the people's preferences as regards their independence and the ownership of the land. We have a situation where the people never lost the land to a foreign invader and in the rural areas the ancient African land tenure system of communal ownership of the land still operates. It is on this peaceful base of security of tenure that one begins to assemble the history of the land.

One has so many options and choices of study that are sure, steady and sane and simply another addition to mankind's history. One can concentrate on the impact of Christianity on the tribes, the power and influence of the missionaries and the London Missionary Society and changing patterns of culture and learning.

Thus, the refrain of recorded history begins very much the way it began in Europe: 'When the Romans first took learning to Europe, the tribes there were just like the tribes of Africa, not knowing anything about learning and progress . . .'

We can look back at the old men, who until the missionaries introduced a new form of learning, were the only libraries the people had and the repositories of all tribal learning and knowledge. We can look back at the earlier religions of the tribes and the persuasive voice of Christianity in modifying and transforming custom and tradition. We can look back on a history that is not sick with the need to exploit and abuse people.

I have found the tensions and balances of the rural parts of Botswana, of a fine order. Enough of the ancient way of African life has survived to enable the younger generations to maintain their balance with comfort and ease, while almost daily with independence, new innovations, new concepts of government and critical, complex situations invade the life of the country. It is in such a world that one puts down some roots in the African soil and one finds a sense of peace about the future.

1984

Foreword to Ellen Kuzwayo's *Call Me Woman*

When the [Afrikaner] Nationalist government first came to power in 1948, they were welcomed in a strange way by black people:

'We prefer the Boer,' they said.

This was said not with any affection for the Boer [Afrikaner], but because he would be a kind of clarifier of the situation in South Africa. The Boer was preferred to the hypocritical English of whom it was said they smiled at you with their front teeth and chewed you with their back teeth. The Boer would hate nakedly, would express his evil and prejudice nakedly and would be a blunt, brutal final death on the land. There would be no half measures. Indeed this was so. With the triumph of Afrikaner Boer

88

power, notices of separate amenities for white and black appeared overnight in public places; a day previously black people had sat wherever they pleased in a bus. Now they were abruptly informed by the driver to move to the back of the bus. It was to be a history of skin colour; skins were to be constantly legislated for, the white skin being a passport to paradise and many privileges; the black skin being a kind of rhinoceros hide at which are hurled tear gas, batons, bullets and ferocious police dogs.

The autobiography of Ellen Kuzwayo puts aside the rhinoceros hide, to reveal a people with a delicate nervous balance like everyone else. No calculation is ever given to the price black people have had to pay for thirty-six years of Boer rule. The documentation of human suffering in this book is terrible. It is as though a death is imposed on people by the ruling white race and black people constantly struggle to survive under this pall of doom. But at the end of the book one feels as if a shadow history of South Africa has been written; there is a sense of triumph, of hope in this achievement and that one has read the true history of the land, a history that vibrates with human compassion and goodness.

Ellen Kuzwayo's lifespan covers two major eras. First comes the era of her youth when, for black people, she could still feel Southern Africa as one cultural unit of traditional moral codes and values and where most black people were rural people who lived on the land as farmers. Her family benefits from a special form of land tenure common to many Barolong clans at the turn of the century whereby the chiefs had divided the land into private farms while technically owning a final protecting right over these farms. In reality the old order has been disrupted and she represents a new generation that is an harmonious blending of traditional courtesies and Christian values. Her youth and education in such institutions as Lovedale College equip her for the beautiful contribution she makes during her lifetime. As a young girl she is taught to serve, not only her immediate family circle but also the passer-by on the highway who might be hungry. Colleges such as Lovedale and Fort Hare were under the control of missionaries and the education was of a high quality. From this educated class of black people, both men and women, there are the first stirrings of political activity, but with a very broad base. It was felt that tribalism was a danger to the black community and that the leadership should be chosen on the basis of merit and not ethnicity. The women accepted a two-fold role, to liberate themselves from a traditional heritage of inferiority and to support the men on issues of national liberation.

The abrupt break Ellen Kuzwayo experiences from an early rural background to the broken disjointed chaos of the slums and shacks of the townships of Johannesburg follows a pattern experienced by many black people. The men are forced off the land to earn money in the mines to pay poll tax. Starving women of the rural areas follow the men to the city and survive precariously, brewing beer or working in domestic service. Of Johannesburg, Soweto, she writes: '. . . it is not easy to live and bring up children in a community robbed of its traditional moral code and values; a community lost between its old heritage and culture and that of its colonists.'

All the headline news is here, the desperate eruptions in Soweto, the bashings, the shootings, the bannings, the detentions and the mass murder of school children in Soweto during the 1976 unrests. Since the rhinoceros hide is put to one side one often puts the book down in agitation, finding it impossible to believe that people could endure such terrific suffering. The truth is the human physical frame cannot endure unnatural states of torture, unnatural states of detention. Ellen Kuzwayo's son, Justice Bakone, is involved in a black consciousness literacy programme. For this community service he is banned to a desolation in Mafikeng and only allowed to speak to one person at a time. He breaks down inwardly. He finds solitude impossible to bear.

During Mrs Kuzwayo's own detention for five months in 1976, we learn that there are two forms of detention for political prisoners. She was detained under Section 10 and allowed newspapers, letters and fresh food from outside prison. Then there's Section 6. One just walks into it and is bashed about by the security police from wall to wall, knocked to the ground, and so on. This is done to young girls aged twelve. One day she heard the terrified inmates of Section 6 sing their Sunday school song: 'Amazing Love'. I cannot see a Lord in the sky who will provide that amazing love, but I can see people providing it for people. That's what this book is all about. Books like these will be the Bible one day for the younger generations.

1985

Some happy memories of Iowa

◆

As the plane from New York neared Cedar Rapids I looked down in surprise at endless stretches of neatly ploughed farmland. It was in such a community that I was to live for four months. It made me review my image of the United States. To the rest of the world the United States would seem to be Hollywood, Washington, New York, Chicago, and Los Angeles, where all the bad things happen. We travelled through Iowa and it was all the same – small towns like Iowa City surrounded by vast stretches of farmland. Strange religious cults quietly lived out their ancient dramas and turned up in shops and restaurants in old-fashioned clothing. A feeling grew in me that whole villages in Europe and England had emigrated two hundred years ago to what was called the 'new world' and kept that village quality of life.

I soon felt happy and at ease in Iowa City. The population was the same as my village, Serowe – 40,000 people. Like my village, the town was small and manageable and I soon found my way around. It was as if I had never left the Serowe post office, when I walked up to the counter clerk and asked for some aerograms.

'I'm sorry,' he said. 'They are out of stock.'

Shopping sometimes gave me problems. American English isn't the British English that is spoken in Southern Africa. I walked into a stationery shop and said to the man behind the counter: 'I would like to buy a rubber, please.'

The man said: 'We don't sell them in ones. We sell them in threes.'

I said: 'But I want only one rubber.'

The man became hostile: 'But I told you we only sell them in threes.'

I said: 'All right, I'll take three then.'

The man walked to the back of the shop and returned with a small packet of prophylactics that he handed to me. He had such a peculiar look in his eyes that I thought he believed I was a prostitute who had suddenly invaded Iowa City. Half fainting with shock I struggled to explain. 'I mean the thing you rub mistakes out with.'

'Oh,' he said. 'You mean an eraser.'

Wherever I live I always build quiet, predictable routines. I already had my breakfast by the time the postman called. I would look out of the window at nine o'clock, see his van, and then go downstairs and wait for him to sort the mail into our mailboxes. On a bench were piles of the university newspaper. It was so peaceful that I would read it absent-mindedly. Things like chicken manure and other farming matters made the daily headlines. Then everything went wrong. Bader was killed in prison and Sadat went to Israel. The chicken manure was swept from the front page for weeks and weeks.

I was researching a historical novel and had partly done some of the work at home. My next chore was to visit the university library. The first time I did so I was thrown off balance. A young man stood behind a counter writing on a card. He looked up briefly. 'Can I help you?' he asked.

My story was a long one. I began: 'I am doing research for a historical novel on Southern Africa . . .'

'Africa,' he said. 'Fifth floor.' And he went back to writing on the card again. I stood there shaking with fright. I am used to libraries where the librarian holds your hand and finds books for you. The young man was completely uninterested in my existence. I took my courage in both hands and took the lift to the fifth floor. Never had I seen such a desolation of solitude, silence, and books. I had never worked in a library like this but in libraries crowded with people. But I soon warmed up to the books when I saw what was there. Anything that had ever been published on Africa was there.

Books long out of print but essential to my research were there. I looked in wonder at an ancient book, *Native Life in South Africa*, by Sol T. Plaatje. It had never been loaned or read. I had to slit open some of the pages in order to read the book. In the words of Jorge Luis Borges: 'Paradise is a library.' The fifth floor became that paradise to me.

I enjoyed meeting the farmers and their wives. One of the farmers' wives prepared a delicious dinner for us. Just as we were about to depart she asked us if we would send her a little sample of our writing. I sent her a love story. A few days later she phoned me. She said she had a women's club and the women were eager to talk to me. Would I come one evening, stay overnight, and let her bring me back to the Mayflower the following day? I agreed.

The woman's club was fascinating to me. There was an American flag on the mantelpiece. Before anything happened the women turned to the flag and said something. Then the chairlady opened procedures.

'We have all read your love story and enjoyed it. Now we are going to talk about love for the Lord.' All the women bowed their heads and she said a little prayer. Then the women looked up at me expectantly. They were bursting with questions, eager to know about the part of the world I came from. I enjoyed this kindness. They lived in a small, quiet, shut-in, conservative world but it could admit other wonders and things.

President John Kennedy had accurately defined the soul of the American nation. 'We are a conservative people,' he said. He must have known about all those little villages in Europe and England that had transported themselves so many years ago to the United States. Villagers are always conservative.

1987

Writing out of Southern Africa

When young people ask me: 'How do I become a writer?' I always reply that a career in writing first begins with love of reading and a love of books, a feeling for all the magic and wonder that can be communicated through books. I can see no other certain beginning for a career so ill-defined in concrete terms with vague language like in-born talent, in-born gift. This unease and uncertainty haunts a writer all throughout his life – that the most recent manuscript is not the masterpiece his other books were, that he was only capable of producing the one great novel and that his talent is dead forever.

I think no writer ever plans a career in writing, an often miserable occupation filled with anguish, mental blocks and physical and mental exhaustion. In the end all that ever tempted one to tread that road of super-human staying power and stamina that is needed to produce the full-length novel, is a love of books itself. This slow unfolding of writing talent is most aptly described by the French writer, Albert Camus: 'So, you think what you have is your own? What is your own comes to you, bit by bit.'

I have struggled with the young at workshops in Botswana about this reading tradition. They express frustration at their inability to produce the great Botswana novel overnight and deflect their attention to neighbouring countries who have had wars of independence. If they had been guerrillas fighting bloody wars, they would produce these great novels. There is nothing inspiring in Botswana with its peaceful history of colonial occupation, so they say.

In reality the country has a unique colonial history as a British Protectorate – the land, the culture and the people survived almost intact and undisturbed. I know of other British protectorates in Africa where the soul of the people was left intact and undisturbed, the British being mainly interested in resources, not the people, but what is unique about Botswana is that over the 80-year period of British occupation, the country produced two leader images – Khama the Great and his son Tshekedi Khama who asserted black pride and independence and claims to the land. They were men admired in Britain and their personalities lay like a protective mantle over the land, right up until Independence. Here you have ancient Africa almost intact but with many subtle blendings of everything new that was introduced to the people over the

94

centuries. Here you have a people who say: 'Since time immemorial we have done this . . .' I have drawn on this depth and stability as a writer.

The world of the intellect

Everything is at a beginning. No colonial power ever intended planning for black majority populations. They planned for themselves alone. Education, schools, were introduced by missionary effort, often in an elementary form. Libraries, schools and planning for people were provided after independence. It could be said that a reading tradition was absent in the society. This is not my background. Having no family to rear me I was reared in part by missionaries and had access to large libraries when young. I view my own activity as a writer as a kind of participation in the thought of the whole world. No other occupation provides for such an international outlook as writing. I have my national, my African side but I am also very much an international kind of person.

Writing is not a male/female occupation. My femaleness was never a problem to me, not now, not in our age. More than a century ago, a few pioneer women writers, writing fearfully under male pseudonyms, established that women writers were brilliant thinkers too, on a par with men. I do not have to be a feminist. The world of the intellect is impersonal, sexless. The young struggle with questions of literacy, nationalism in Africa. It is constructive to outline to the young the road one has travelled, the themes one has worked on in one's private workshop and the way in which life conspired to make one a writer. I have worked outside all political and other ideologies, bowing to life here and there and absorbing all that I felt to be relevant, but always fighting for space and air. I needed this freedom and independence, in order that I retain a clarity of thought, in order that my sympathies remain fluent and responsive to any given situation in life. I offer a brief outline of my major themes, the major shaping influences in my life.

A bit of Christianity

I was steeped in it when young and have a thorough acquaintance with the bible and the life of Jesus Christ but Christianity and formal church going were never going to be an expansive way of life for me. However, I value my early background and training with its ideal service to life. I value that vivid, great short story teller, Jesus Christ, and the foundation he laid for such terms as mankind, the human race and love of one's neighbour.

It was a question often asked of him: 'Lord, who is my neighbour?' And he would reply with a little story about a Jew who was attacked on the highway by robbers. Many Jews passed by and ignored the injured man until a Samaritan chanced by and offered assistance of all kinds to the injured man. Or he would tell about being thirsty at a well and a foreign woman, not a Jewish woman, would offer him a drink of water. It was as if, from then onwards, individual thinkers and philosophers expanded on this theme. Mankind never began as mankind but as small tribal groups and nations.

I accept as valid a proposition made by an American anthropologist, Ruth Benedict, that the roots of racial prejudice and nationalism go deep. In her book *Patterns Of Culture*, she writes:

> Now modern man has made this thesis (our own local ways) one of the living issues in his thought and in his practical behaviour, but the sources of it go far back into what appears to be, from its universal distribution among primitive peoples, one of the earliest of human distinctions, the difference in kind between 'my own' closed group and the outsider. All primitive tribes agree in recognising this category of the outsiders, those who are not only outside the provisions of the moral code which holds within the limits of one's own people, but who are summarily denied a place anywhere in the human scheme.
>
> A great number of tribal names in common use, Zuni, Dene, Kiowa, and the rest, are names by which primitive peoples know themselves, and are only their native terms for 'the human beings', that is, themselves. Outside of the closed group there are no human beings. And this is in spite of the fact that from an

objective point of view each tribe is surrounded by peoples sharing in its arts and material inventions, in elaborate practices that have grown up by a mutual give-and-take of behaviour from one people to another. Primitive man never looked out over the world and saw mankind. From the beginning he was a provincial who raised the barriers high. Whether it was a question of choosing a wife or of taking a headman, the first and most important distinction was between his own human group and those beyond the pale. His own group, and all its ways of behaving, was unique.

A bit of Pan-Africanism

That primitive way of life, outlined above, 'we the human beings, our closed group outside of which there are no human beings,' underlies the social order of South Africa. There is only one race of humans there, the white race. Anything black or tainted with black has been abhorred, detested, reviled, abused and exploited. My personal feeling is that people, when faced with a power structure that attempts to destroy their humanity, find ways and means of keeping their humanity intact. I feel that the older generations used Christianity to keep their humanity intact because we were all faced with generations of older people who were pious, humble, deferential and saintly Christians.

The African National Congress, which is now so militant, was once an expression of that humble deference. The ANC received a shaking-up in the 1950s when Robert Sobukwe broke away from their youth wing to found the Pan Africanist Congress. Sobukwe's view was Pan African and he personally included all things African, but with an edge of harshness that forced one to make an identification with Africa and a sense of belonging to Africa. That edge of harshness was all right for me. Like most black people born in South Africa, I lived with a very broken sense of history. A very brief encounter with Robert Sobukwe helped me to adjust and get a sense of balance. He gave me a comfortable black skin in which to live and work. Apart from this slight acquaintance with the world of politics and power, I have carefully avoided politics and power, both in a personal capacity and in my work. My world is a quiet backwater where ideas and inventions dominate and where people have time to love each other.

The inspiration of Bertolt Brecht

Sometimes a book burns its way into one's mind and is never forgotten. This was so with an early biography I read of the German playwright, Bertolt Brecht – *A Choice of Evils* – published in 1960. The biography divided Brecht's life into three main phases:

There was Brecht, the gay young man who produced the *Three Penny Opera* and who could turn the whole city of Berlin upside down.

There was Brecht, after he had read *Das Kapital* and became the great convert to Marxism.

There was Brecht in his exile in the United States during the Hitler era and his final return to Berlin.

It was the middle phase that fascinated me. It was Germany between the two world wars when the Deutsche Mark was so inflated that it could hardly purchase a box of matches. Brecht applied his mind to creating a new social order. He began to produce the didactic, teaching plays. He had students of the University of Berlin research for him how a whole town could be re-shaped along Marxist lines. He would sit in a room full of students and have each student read out his research. From a consensus of opinion he would shape the didactic plays. They could read like an educational sing-song:

In this town we will have so many schools. In these schools we will have so many pupils. In these schools we will teach the following subjects . . .

Brecht came from a poor peasant background. With him ordinary mankind came into his own and he was the rich, creative artist who could make a dry and difficult doctrine like Marxism live. Ordinary people are full of ribald fun and humour and in Brecht this promise was always there – that it would be fun to reshape the world. There is in me the same love for counting chairs and tables and planning for people, with the same promise of fun and unpredictable humour.

Experiments with the new

My life spans two countries in Southern Africa, South Africa and Botswana. I acquired my education in South Africa but wrote all my books in Serowe, Botswana. When I arrived in the village of Serowe in 1964, the people were about to engage in a gigantic co-operative and educational project. It was inspired by the man, Patrick van Rensburg, who had resigned from the South African diplomatic service and who wished to make a constructive contribution to Southern Africa. But the people of Serowe had been engaged like this in the past under their chiefs, and been very independently concerned with their own progress. The people would experiment with anything – new ideas for educational progress, new agricultural techniques, new anything. It was a phase that lasted eleven years and then ceased abruptly. But I recorded everything, counting tables and chairs in great detail. It was Bertolt Brecht who gave me the courage to write like that.

A reverence for people

A discipline I have observed is an attitude of love and reverence to people. I have used the word God, in a practical way, in my books. I cannot find a substitute word for all that is most holy but I have tried to deflect people's attention into offering to each other what they offer to an Unseen Being in the sky. When people are holy to each other, war will end, human suffering will end.

It is rather its spiritual side that concerns me. I believe that all the nations of the earth are drawing closer to each other. I deal in human grandeur as a writer and recognise it when I see it. I would propose that mankind will one day be ruled by men who are God and not greedy, power-hungry politicians. I see this achievement as not the effort of a single man but a collaboration of many great minds in order that an integrity be established in the affairs of men. Only then can the resources of the earth be cared for and shared in an equitable way among all mankind.

Hand in hand with world government I clearly foresee a new race of people – not nations or national identity as such but rather people who are a blending of all the nations of the earth. Its beginnings are already there so I do not see any of this as being forced on people, but that it is the natural outcome of mankind's slow spiritual unfoldment over the centuries. These are the themes that have preoccupied me as a writer.

1985

Epilogue: An African Story

It was a winter morning. Just before dawn the stars shone like bright, polished blue jewels in the sky and a half-eclipsed moon suddenly arose with a hauntingly beautiful light. And it was a summer afternoon. The summer rain had filled my yard with wild flowers. I seemed to be living too, all the time, with animals' eyes — goats staring at me, cows staring at me, chickens staring at me. I slowly came alive with the background scenery. What have I said about the people of a free land, I who borrowed their clothes, their goats, their sunrises and sunsets for my books? Not anything very polite, it seems.

The wandering travellers of ancient times came unexpectedly upon people sitting around their outdoor fires.

'Who are you?' people asked.

'I am the dreamer and storyteller,' they replied. 'I have seen life. I am drunk with the magical enchantment of human relationships. I laughed often. The big, wide free world is full of innocence . . .'

One imagines that those people always welcomed the storytellers. Each human society is a narrow world, trapped to death in paltry evils and jealousies, and for people to know that there are thoughts and generosities wider and freer than their own can only be an enrichment to their lives. But what happens to the dreamer and storyteller when he is born into a dead world of such extreme cruelties that no comment or statement of love can alter them? In the first place, in South Africa, who is one talking to? People there are not people but complexions and hair textures — whites, Coloureds, Indians and Africans. Who can write about that? Where is that wedge of innocence and laughter that resolves so many human ills?

It has surprised me, the extent to which creative writing is often regarded, unconsciously, as a nationalistic activity, and perhaps this expression of national feeling is rather the subdued communication a writer holds with his own society. I have so often been referred to as 'the Botswana writer', while in reality the Botswana

101

personality isn't as violent as me. I wasn't born with the gentle inquiring eyes of a cow but amongst black people who always said, when anything went wrong: 'Why don't we all die?' And the subdued undertone was: 'since the white man hates us so much.'

Thought patterns change rapidly from one generation to another. We reformed the language of our parents because once the white man in South Africa started putting up notices 'For whites only', he also dispensed with normal human decencies – like 'please' and 'thank you' and 'I'm sorry' – while black people retained theirs as they have no benches to defend. It is impossible to translate a scene like this into human language. I once sat down on a bench at Cape Town railway station where the notice 'Whites Only' was obscured. A few moments later a white man approached and shouted: 'Get off!' It never occurred to him that he was achieving the opposite of his dreams of superiority and had become a living object of contempt, that human beings, when they are human, dare not conduct themselves in such ways.

It is preferable to have the kind of insecurity about life and death that is universal to man: *I am sure of so little*. It is despicable to have this same sense of insecurity – especially about a white skin – defended by power and guns. It seems to remove from them all fear of retribution for their deeds and it creates in the recipient of their wild, fierce, savage cruelty a deep sense of shock.

Day after day one hears of unbelievable slaughter in Ireland. A traveller from England passed my way. 'Why are people being killed like that in Ireland?' I asked. 'The Catholics are fighting for their rights,' he said. 'They have always been discriminated against, never allowed to purchase their own homes and things like that. It's just like South Africa. There they call it racialism. In Ireland they call it religion.'

Every oppressed man has this suppressed violence, as though silently awaiting the time to set right the wrongs that afflict him. I have never forgotten it, even though, for the purposes of my trade, I borrowed the clothes of a country like Botswana.

South Africa made white people rich and comfortable, but their ownership of the country is ugly and repellent. They talk about South Africa in tourist language all the time: 'This grand and

102

sunny land,' they say. The cheap, glaring, paltry trash of a people who are living it up for themselves alone dominates everything, infiltrates everywhere. If one is a part of it, through being born there, how does one communicate with the horrible? That is why South Africa has no great writer: no one can create harmony out of cheap discord.

It is impossible to guess how the revolution will come one day in South Africa. But in a world where all ordinary people are insisting on their rights, it is inevitable. It is to be hoped that great leaders will arise there who remember the suffering of racial hatred and out of it formulate a common language of human love for all people.

Possibly too, Southern Africa might one day become the home of the storyteller and dreamer, who did not hurt others but only introduced new dreams that filled the heart with wonder.

1972

CHRONOLOGY

1937   (6 July) Bessie Amelia Emery born Pietermaritzburg, Natal, South Africa. Goes into foster care.

1943   Death of mother.

1950   Placed in Anglican mission orphanage in Durban. Attends high school. Trains as primary school teacher.

1957–59   Works as primary school teacher.

1959–60   Works for *Golden City Post* (later *Post*) on *Home Post* Supplement.

1960   Moves to Cape Town.

1962   Marries journalist Harold Head.

1963   Moves briefly to Port Elizabeth, back to Cape Town. Howard Head born.

1964   Estranged from husband.
              (March) Leaves South Africa on exit permit for Serowe, Botswana. Assumes primary school teaching post.

1964–65   Drought in Botswana.

1966   (30 September) Botswana becomes independent.
              When Rain Clouds Gather commissioned by Simon and Schuster.
              Moves to Francistown as refugee.

1967   Moves back to Serowe.
              When Rain Clouds Gather published, Simon and Schuster, New York.
              Onset of mental illness. Certified, admitted to psychiatric hospital, Gaborone.

1970   Recovery.

1971   *Maru* published, Victor Gollancz, London.

1972   *Serowe: Village of the Rain Wind* commissioned by Penguin.

1973   *A Question of Power* published, Davis-Poynter, London.

1977   *The Collector of Treasures* published, Heinemann, London.

Applies unsuccessfully for Botswanan citizenship.
(Sept.)–1978 (Jan.) Attends International Writing
Program in Iowa, USA.

1979 Granted Botswanan citizenship.
(22 June – 15 July) Travels to Berlin for Horizons '79
Africa Festival.

1981 *Serowe: Village of the Rain Wind* published, David
Philip, Cape Town and Heinemann, London.

1982 (May) Travels to Gaborone to deliver special lecture
and participate in book-signing.

1984 *A Bewitched Crossroad* published, Ad. Donker,
Johannesburg.
(March) Travels to Australia.

1986 (17 April) Dies in Serowe of hepatitis, aged 49.

EDITORIAL NOTE

The original publication details and sequence of the pieces
included in this volume are given below. Minor liberties were taken
with the publication sequence: for example 'The isolation of "Boeta
L." ' was published four months before 'Snowball: a story', and
'Writing out of Southern Africa' two years before 'Some happy
memories of Iowa'. In the first case, 'Snowball: a story' describes
life in District Six and therefore clearly belongs with the other
pieces from this period. In the second, 'Some happy memories of
Iowa', although it appeared in 1987, actually describes a period
several years earlier. 'Writing out of Southern Africa' also has a
consummative quality which makes it an ideal concluding piece.
Changes were made to the original publication sequence in these
and other instances in the interests of a more logical and coherent
narrative structure.

Original publication details

1 Let me tell a story now . . . *The New African* 1.9(1962): 8–9.
2 An unspeakable crime. *The New African* 2.1(1963): 11.
3 A gentle people: the warm, uncommitted 'Coloureds' of the
   Cape. *The New African* 2.8(1963): 169–170.
4 Letter from South Africa: for a friend, 'D.B.'. *Transition*
   11.3(1963): 40.
5 Gladys Mgudlandlu: the exuberant innocent. *The New
   African* 2.10(1963): 209.
6 The isolation of 'Boeta L.': Atteridgeville in 1964. *The New
   African* 3.2(1964): 28–29.
7 Snowball: a story. *The New African* 3.5(1964): 100–101.
8 Letter to *Transition*. *Transition* 17.4(1964): 6.
9 For Serowe: a village in Africa. *The New African* 4.10(1965):
   230.
10 The woman from America. *New Statesman* 26 August 1966:
   287.
11 Chibuku beer and independence. *The New African*
   5.9(1966): 200.

12 Village people. *Classic* 2.3(1967): 19–20.

13 The old woman. *Classic* 2.3(1967): 20–21.

14 God and the underdog: thoughts on the rise of Africa. *The New African* 7.2(1968): 47–48.

15 African religions. *The New African* No.53(Nov.1969): 46–47.

16 An African story. *The Listener* 30 November 1972: 735–736.

17 Reply to questionnaire on the South African cultural boycott. *Index on Censorship* 4.2(1975): 23.

18 Preface to 'Witchcraft'. *Ms*. Vol.4(1975): 72–73.

19 Despite broken bondage, Botswana women are still unloved. *The Times*(London) 13 August 1975: 5.

20 Makeba music. *Donga* No.4(1977): 6.

21 Some notes on novel writing. *New Classic* No.5(1978): 30–32.

22 Social and political pressures that shape literature in Southern Africa. *World Literature Written in English* 18.1(1979): 20–26.

23 A note on *Rain Clouds*. *Gar*(Feb.1979): 27.

24 Notes from a quiet backwater. *Drum*(Feb.1982): 35–36.

25 Foreword to Sol Plaatje's *Native Life in South Africa*. Johannesburg: Ravan, 1982: ix–xiii.

26 The old iron cooking pot of Europe. *LIP from Southern African Women*. Eds. Susan Brown, Isabel Hofmeyr and Susan Rosenberg. Johannesburg: Ravan, 1983: 5–7.

27 A search for historical continuity and roots. *Momentum: On Recent Southern African Writing*. Eds. M.J. Daymond, J.U. Jacobs, Margaret Lenta. Pietermaritzburg:Natal UP, 1984: 278–80.

28 Writing out of Southern Africa. *New Statesman* 15 August 1985: 21–23.

29 Foreword to Ellen Kuzwayo's *Call Me Woman*. Johannesburg: Ravan, 1985: xiii–xv.

30 Some happy memories of Iowa. *The World Comes to Iowa: Iowa International Anthology*. Eds. Paul Engle, Rowena Torrevillas, Hualing Nieh Engle. Iowa: Iowa State UP, 1987: 86–88.